D1559994

DEATH
&
BEYOND

DEATH

&

BEYOND

by Andrew Greeley

THE THOMAS MORE PRESS
Chicago, Illinois

Acknowledgments

For permission to quote from the sources indicated below, the publishers and author express their thanks:

From *Islam, Muhammad and His Religion,* edited by Arthur Jeffrey, Copyright © 1958, by the Liberal Arts Press, Inc., reprinted by permission of the Bobbs-Merrill Company, Inc.

From *Parapsychological Monographs No. 8.,* "Paranormal Phenomena, Science, and Life after Death," by C. J. Ducasse. Copyright © 1969 by the Parapsychology Foundation, New York, N.Y.

From *Spiritual Frontiers,* Autumn and Winter, 1974, "Some Frontiers in Survival Research" by Karlis Osis. Copyright © 1974 American Society for Psychical Research, New York, N.Y.

From *An Anthology of Irish Literature* by David H. Greene, © 1971 by New York University. Reprinted by permission of New York University Press.

From *The Collected Poems of G. K. Chesterton,* Copyright 1932 by Dodd, Mead & Company, Inc. Copyright renewed 1960 by Oliver Chesterton. Reprinted by permission of the publishers.

From *The ESP Reader,* edited by David C. Knight. Copyright © 1969 by Grosset & Dunlap, Inc. Used by permission of the publishers.

From *The Romeo Error: A Matter of Life and Death* by Lyall Watson. Copyright © 1974 by Lyall Watson. Reprinted by permission of Doubleday & Co., Inc.

CONTENTS

Prefatory Note

In the first two chapters I deal with "limit-" or "horizon-experience." I discuss "reassurance" in the next four chapters and "reflection" in the final two.

Chapter 1

RITE OF SPRING

WE MUST BEGIN WITH SIGHTS AND SOUNDS. LET US SWITCH on the turntable. Solti and the Chicago Symphony play Stravinsky's "Rite of Spring." It is wild, savage, barbaric, violent, destructive, sublime, peaceful, joyous, glorious music. The spring of Stravinsky and Solti is not the idyllic, bucolic spring of Victorian poetry; it is not the peaceful, gentle, sweet spring of the romantic imagination; it is not the sentimental, sticky spring of popular love songs. It is a passionate, violent, potentially destructive spring. Life erupts at springtime violently and even dangerously.

In "The Wasteland," T. S. Eliot considers April to be "the cruellest month:"

> April is the cruellest month, breeding
> Lilacs out of the dead land, mixing
> Memory and desire, stirring
> Dull roots with spring rain.

Anyone who has walked in the woods (at least in the northeastern and middle western part of the country) in March or April, even May, knows how accurate Eliot's description is. April in middle western America is at least a month behind Eliot's, but the struggle, the anguish, the labor pains of nature striving to give birth can still be seen. The thick, oozing mud, the rapidly flowing, almost angry, waters of the creek, the fierce winds blowing in from the southwest, the last traces of melting snow, the waves of the lake pounding the debris-littered shore, the browns, grays, whites of the earth and the alternating blue and lowering, rapidly moving clouds, the rotted leaves of last autumn, the bodies of animals who have not survived the winter lying uncovered now and vulnerable to the ravages of rain and sun, the trees torn from the earth by early spring storms, drab and ugly fields, and everywhere mud, mud, mud. Something may well be coming to life, but it is not done easily; there is much pain and death in evidence as life struggles to be reborn.

April turns into May, and we turn from Eliot to Gerard Manley Hopkins whose "The May Magnificat" describes the almost lunatic superabundance, the wild, chaotic disorderly vitality that suddenly takes possession of the earth:

> May is Mary's month, and I
> Muse at that and wonder why:
>   Her feasts follow reason,
>   Dated due to season—
>
> Candlemas, Lady Day;
> But the Lady Month, May,
>   Why fasten that upon her,
>   With a feasting in her honour?
>
> Is it only its being brighter
> Than the most are must delight her?
>   Is it opportunest
>   And flower finds soonest?
>
> Ask of her, the mighty mother:
> Her reply puts this other
>   Question: What is Spring?—
>   Growth in every thing—
>
> Flesh and fleece, fur and feather,
> Grass and greenworld all together;

Star-eyed strawberry-breasted
Throstle above her nested

Cluster of bugle blue eggs thin
Forms and warms the life within;
  And bird and blossom swell
  In sod or sheath or shell.

All things rising, all things sizing
Mary sees, sympathising
  With the world of good,
  Nature's motherhood.

Their magnifying of each its kind
With delight calls to mind
  How she did in her stored
  Magnify the Lord.

Well but there was more than this:
Spring's universal bliss
  Much, had much to say
  To offering Mary May.

When drops-of-blood-and foam-dapple
Bloom lights the orchard-apple
  And thicket and thorp are merry
  With silver-surfed cherry

And azuring-over greybell makes
Wood banks and brakes wash wet like lakes
  And magic cuckoo call
  Caps, clear, and clinches all—

This ecstasy all through mothering earth
Tells Mary her mirth till Christ's birth
  To remember and exultation
  In God who was her salvation.

Life does not emerge in the spring with neat, orderly restraint. It bursts forth, it breaks into the open, it overflows, it surges in all directions. The grass, trees, bushes, plants, flowers, fields, birds, animals all seem to surge back into existence at the same moment. Spring is like a group of primary grade students let loose at recess. They explode out of the school building, dash in all directions, screaming at the top of their lungs. Spring does not come quietly; it erupts.

Yet the eruption of life in the spring is also linked with death. We know that what is born with the spring will die in the cold of the following autumn and winter; that which has come into being will eventually be buried, that which is surging with vitality will become rotten and corrupt. The green fields will become brown and gray again, the songs of the birds will be stilled, the flowers will wither and die. Indeed, that which is blooming now is living off the corruption and decay of that which lived in the past. The rotting rubble of old life is absorbed in the fresh surge of new life. The sun rises and sets, and by its setting gives birth to itself again next morning.

> For birth hath in itself the germ of death,
>   But death hath in itself the germ of birth.
> It is the falling acorn buds the tree,
> The falling rain that bears the greenery,
>   The fern-plants moulder when the ferns arise.
>   For there is nothing lives but something dies,
> And there is nothing dies but something lives.
>   Till skies be fugitives,
> Till Time, the hidden root of change, updries,
> Are Birth and Death inseparable on earth;
> For they are twain yet one, and Death is Birth.
>
>   —Francis Thompson
>   "Ode to the Setting Sun"

It is not merely that death is a prelude to birth; death is the price that must be paid for birth. The maiden must die in Stravinsky's "Rite of Spring." Human sacrifice, as the price paid to the gods to guarantee fertility in the field, is as old as agriculture itself. The Aztecs in Mexico developed this bizarre bargaining with their gods to its ultimate horror.

The followers of Montezuma may have distorted the insight beyond all recognition, but there is still no denying its fundamental truth: Life and death are inextricably linked. "For there is nothing lives but something dies,/And there is nothing dies but something lives." The violent, superabundant outburst of spring defies death, but dying is the price of defiance. The ancient Christian Easter hymn, *Victimae Paschali*, tells the same theme: Jesus had to die in order that he might rise again.

The oldest human civilizations we know believed that spring was a "sacrament," a revelation of the fundamental powers and forces at work in the universe. There is no religion in the world that does not have a rite of spring, a ritual celebrating the rebirth of nature, a festival asserting the triumph of life over death. Easter, the Christian feast of the resurrection of Jesus, is nothing more than a Christian spring festival. While the content of that which is revealed by the Christian rite of spring is very different from that of other religions, the symbol in which the Christian revelation is incarnate is part of the common human religious tradition. Spring means life—violent, superabundant, overflowing life. Life is reborn passionately, madly, gloriously; but life is purchased at the cost of death.

Did Jesus really rise from the dead? Whatever decision we may ultimately make on that question on the basis of religious faith, we still must admit the question is historically unanswerable.

An immense amount of time and energy has been poured into the futile effort of trying to "prove" with historical argument the "fact" of the resurrection of Jesus—or to disprove the "fact" with counterarguments. The modern historian, whatever his personal belief, must say that on the basis of the canons of his discipline the data are inconclusive. You may choose to believe in the resurrection; you cannot "prove" it.

But it is not only the modern historian who rejects "proof" of the resurrection. The early Christian preachers did not attempt to prove the fact of the resurrection; they merely proclaimed it and invited faith. The very nature of the event is such that proof is impossible. You may be able to prove what happened at Pearl Harbor, Watergate, or the St. Bartholomew's Day massacre, or the storming of the Tuilleries. You can't prove what happened outside the city walls of Jerusalem on the first day of the week after the Passover in the year 30. Something extraordinary did indeed happen, but the nature of the event necessarily escapes all scientific human analysis. It would have been much better if all the energy devoted to proving or disproving the fact of the resurrection had been expanded on efforts to understand what the Easter event *means*.

History tells us that something extraordinary happened after the death of Jesus. His followers experienced him as still alive. There is no other explanation for the beginning of Christianity. The followers were not brave or talented or zealous people. They became missionaries of a new faith despite themselves. "Passover plots," "grave robberies," and other similar farfetched explanations are dismissed by most competent historians. Something happened, and that something transformed the followers of Jesus. If that "some-thing" was a form of self-deception, it was surely the most extraordinary and deeply-rooted unconscious self-deception in human history.

The precise nature of the event escapes historical analysis. Most Scripture scholars now agree that the New Testament accounts are later attempts to explain the event and are not historically precise "instant replays" of what happened. The committed Christian believes, of course, that Jesus really and truly rose from the dead, but the physiological and psychological nature of the event is no clearer to faith than to history. The historian says something happened; the believer claims to know what happened, but even he cannot make any legitimate claim to know *how* it happened.

I once heard two very distinguished Catholic theologians engage in a foolish argument as to whether if there were a TV camera at the entrance of the tomb it would have recorded the resurrection of Jesus. One said it would have, the other argued that it would not. I could not escape the irreverent fantasy of Frank Gifford, Howard Cosell, and Dandy Don Meredith describing the event (in the pre-Alex Karas days). Indeed, I could hear Dandy say, "It sure is good to have old Jesus back with us again, isn't it Howard?"

The argument was absurd. There was no TV camera at the entrance to the tomb, and no witnesses were there to record what happened. The followers of Jesus believed that he was still alive, and even they did not try to describe how it was that he still lived. Some contemporary Christians, in a misguided zeal to debate rationally, try to explain what their ancient predecessors knew was ultimately beyond explanation.

We should therefore abandon arguments about the *how* of the resurrection and turn to the *why*. What does Easter mean? Was the resurrection simply a clever magic trick which God produced to refute his enemies? Was it the ultimate debating point to be used in arguments with agnostics, rationalists, and atheists? Did God in His wisdom anticipate the religious debates of the twentieth century and cause the resurrection to be put into the hands of the Christian apologists as the ace of trumps? Is the resurrection a blue chip for Christians to use in dialogue with unbelievers? Merely to ask these questions indicates how foolish has been our approach to the resurrection of Jesus.

The resurrection is a symbol. This does not mean that it is a fairy story, or a legend, or something that is not real. Indeed there is nothing more real than a symbol, for a symbol is a "sacrament." (The word in Latin and Greek means both "symbol" and "sacrament," in fact.) A symbol is a reality that tells us about another and deeper reality. The flag is a symbol of America because it stands for and reveals to us the nation and its political ideals. Religious symbols are stories which tell us about the way things *really* are, about the meaning of human life and of human death, about the purpose of the universe, about good and evil, love and hatred. A religious symbol tells us about God and man and the relationship between the two. Sometimes the story may be just a pious fiction, but in the Jewish and Christian religious traditions, the symbol is a story about something that actually happened. The event that happened is not an end in itself; it is rather designed to reveal to us the nature of God and the meaning of human life. The resurrection, in other words, is not a fact to be argued about; it is a "secret" (to use St. Paul's word) to be probed, a "mystery" (another translation for St. Paul's word) to be understood, a "revelation" by which we are illumined. The critical question for a Christian who believes in the resurrection, and also for the non-Christian who wants to know the essence of the Christian faith, is what does the resurrection of Jesus tell the Christian about the nature of God and the purpose of human life?

To answer that question we must remember, first of all, that Easter and the Jewish feast of Passover are spring festivals. Even before the Jews encountered Yahweh in the desert around Sinai, the Feast of the Unleavened Bread and the Feast of the Spring Lamb were celebrations of the rebirth of life at the end of the winter and the beginning of the spring season. The Passover was always a celebration of life the Children of Israel experienced when they escaped from Egypt. Every religion the world knows has a spring festival to celebrate the rebirth of nature after the long death of winter. The source of the spring celebrations is the mysterious link between life and death, death and life. At those times, humankind makes explicit its wonder about the meaning of its own death.

We see death all around us. Plants, animals, friends, family all die. We know, too, that we will die; but as we witness the glorious rebirth of nature in springtime, we inevitably ask ourselves, is death the ultimate and final end; does it have the last word to say about our life? In the depths of the human unconscious, rooted in the very fibers of the human personality, is the unshakable conviction that life is not without meaning or purpose, that somehow we will be able to conquer death. We know from the research done on "sudden death" experiences that at the moment before "certain" death, peace, serenity, joy, and confidence permeate the personality. Psychoanalysts tell us that the unconscious believes itself immortal. We may rationally reject the hope and confidence at the core of our being; it may well be a deception, the last trick, the ultimate deception of a vindictive, cruel, and arbitrary universe. But the decisive religious question, perhaps the only religious question that ever really matters, is whether that hope which is at the center of our personality is cruel deception or whether it is a hint of an explanation, a rumor of angels, the best single insight we have into what human life is all about. Wherever in the world human beings have celebrated spring, they have asked themselves that question. Their reason may fequently dismiss hope as "wish fulfillment," but that doesn't make hope go away.

Easter is the Christian spring festival. It asks a question as old as humankind. It does not even provide a new answer; there always has been a strong hunch in human nature that death does not say the final word. What the Christian spring feast adds is the power of its certainty that death is not ultimate. The resurrection of Jesus says to the Christian, and through him the rest of humankind, "Dream your most impossible dreams, fantasize your maddest fantasies, hope your wildest hopes, and when they all come to an end what the heavenly Father has prepared for you only begins, for eye has not seen nor has ear heard, nor has it entered into the heart of man what God has prepared for those who love him."

This may not be the way things really are. The data are inconclusive. Life may well be absurd, the universe random chance, existence without purpose. My point is that the resurrection of Jesus "symbolizes" for the Christian the unshakable conviction that the hope which is central in our

personalities is correct; the resurrection is the revelation that
it is all right to hope.

For many Christians this may seem to be a minimal statement of their faith, but I would suggest that it is the core
of the faith from which everything else flows. What is
harder to believe—that one man rose from the dead or that
life triumphs over death for everyone? The resuscitation of
one human is considered an extraordinary occurrence, but
however marvelous it may be it is, after all, only one person.
But the survival of life in its battle with death, the survival
of the life of each one of us, despite death, is an astonishing,
extraordinary, incredible, immense, overwhelming phenomenon. One can, with difficulty perhaps, accept the return to
life of a single person, but the return of life to everyone?
That is a staggering thought.

But that is what the resurrection means. It is important
for a Christian not merely or not even mainly because it
tells of one man whose followers experienced him as alive
after his death, but because it claims to imply the survival of
everyone despite death.

It is much easier to waste time in endless arguments
about the physical details of the resurrection of Jesus because we are not forced thereby to face the overwhelming
challenge of what the resurrection purports to reveal to us
about the nature of the universe, the relationship of God
with man, and the meaning of human life.

The resurrection, then, did not occur to "prove" anything; it occurred—if it occurred at all—to tell us something. We argue about proofs because we do not want to
have to face the challenge in what it tells us.

It is not easy to believe that we can trust our hopeful
instincts. Some people who fancy themselves "modern"

say that they simply cannot accept the resurrection of Jesus. If you believe in modern science, they say, then you have to write the resurrection off as beyond belief. Implicit in such a stance is the assumption that our superstitious ancestors —one step beyond howling savagery—found it easy to believe in the resurrection. Skepticism was not born with the advent of modern science. Belief in the resurrection and all the resurrection implies requires an immense leap of faith for everyone, be he sophisticated modern scientist or illiterate peasant. Belief in the resurrection means belief in one's own survival despite death, it means belief in the correctness of our own irradicable hopefulness. You don't need a Ph.D. in science to find it hard to be hopeful. There is ugliness, suffering, and misery in the universe; life frequently seems to be a ghastly joke, and human events seem often enough to be under the control of a cruel and vicious fate. Though the data are inconclusive, they often seem to "tilt" toward despair.

The spring message, reinforced and revalidated by the story of Jesus, seems hopelessly naive: Life is not the ultimate reality, death is. Birth is the beginning of a brief and futile struggle between two oblivions. Our predecessors were just as likely to form such conclusions as modern, scientifically trained contemporaries. But there is still the miracle of spring, still laughter, still joy, still celebration, still hope. Hints, signals, "rumors"—try as we might to erase them, our hope persists in their existence. The story that Jesus was dead and now lives is believed by Christians as a validation of that hope.

It is a mistake to think, as many Christians seem to, that Jesus was an actor playing a part. They would believe that he went up to Jerusalem knowing that he was going to die with a precise and clear notion of how the heavenly Father was going to validate his preaching. He went through the act, played his part, saw the drama to its end. There was a day or two of anxiety, perhaps, a few hours of acute suffering, and then triumph.

One could admire the acting skill of someone who played such a role, though one could hardly identify with him, because we all go to our own deaths full of fear, hesitancy, and uncertainty. We may be confident that death is not the end, but we are still terrified at the prospect. If we read the New Testament carefully, we see that this was the case for Jesus too. He knew that the heavenly Father would confirm his preaching. He knew it with a greater and a different kind of knowledge than the rest of us possess, but he was not an actor playing a part; he was a human who shared the terror that we all have when faced with death.

It is the Christian conviction that Jesus is the Word of God. By this the Christian means that God speaks to us through the life and death and the new life of Jesus in a special and unique way. He speaks to us, of course, in all of His creation, particularly through our fellow humans. But Jesus, while he was human like us, was also someone "special" (and the greatest problem of Christianity is to explain the nature of that specialness). Jesus was special precisely because God's Word was spoken through him. In the life, the death, and new life of Jesus, God reveals to us what human existence is all about. In a way, one might even say that God "cheats," for Jesus represents an intervention in human events that was not "preprogrammed"; it was something extraordinarily unique, a special revelation that did not have to be, a revelation designed to confirm our wildest hopes.

Let it be clear, then, what Easter means to Christians. It is not a denial of death, it is not a pollyanna pretense that there is no suffering or ugliness or tragedy or absurdity in the universe. Easter represents the Christian acceptance of the fact of death in all its ugliness. It represents the Christian's assertion that there is evil aplenty in the world, but nature is reborn in the springtime, the sun rises every morning, we are reborn every time we experience a decisive personality growth. So the Christian believes through the revelation in the resurrection of Jesus that death does not have the final word and that evil will not have the final victory. Easter morning conveys a very simple message: Life is *almost* a complete and tragic disaster but not quite. At the very last second, the tragedy of human life is turned into comedy, and the existence of the human personality and the human race has a happy ending.

Chapter 2

THE ULTIMATE QUESTION

I HAVE BEGUN WITH EXPERIENCE AND SYMBOL. I HAVE TRIED to call to the reader's mind his experience of spring. Even the most jaded of us urbanites have experienced spring, though often, perhaps, with our peripheral vision. We need the music of Stravinsky and the poetry of Eliot to focus our attention on a phenomenon that was inescapably central to the attention of our archaic ancestors. Spring to them was a matter of life and death in several different senses of the phrase. It not only spoke to them about life and death; it could actually mean their life or their death. A late frost, excessive rains, no rains at all—any of these could quite literally mean death. The ritual sacrifices of spring were a form of hedging the bet. One believed the gods were good, one believed that they would bring nature back to life in the spring, but one had to be sure. The sacrifices were a frequently gruesome way of allaying anxiety. Now, in a world which has suddenly discovered a possibility of massive food shortage, the coming of spring on schedule is important again; but we are still more likely to learn about it from the meteorologist on television than from watching the first shoots of the weed plants push their way through the soil. Yet we do observe the advance of spring. We see the trees turn green, we feel the warm breezes, notice the days lengthening, and worry again about the dandelions on the lawn and cutting the grass. We may not experience spring very intensely, but we do experience it.

Voltaire superciliously announced that humankind
creates God in his own image and likeness. Agnostic pro-
fessors have echoed that ironic line for a couple of centuries.
Human beings try to find some meaning in their lives, and
because they are afraid to concede the absurdity of existence
they fantasize about a god who can protect them from the
harsh realities of an empty, scientific universe. The gods,
religion, "life after death" are all the result of human wish
fulfillment. It sounds so tough-minded, so objective, so
dispassionate, hard-headed. Primitive man was superstitious;
he needed religion, which grew out of his dreams, his fantasies, his ignorance. Contemporary secular man, on the
other hand, is too intelligent to permit himself superstition
and too clear-eyed to permit escape in religious fantasy.
"Modern man" has evolved from the sacred to the profane,
from the religious to the secular. Religion, God, immortality
are to be consigned to the evolutionary ash can.

I begin with experience because religion begins with experience—not doctrine, catechisms, controversy, or fantasy.
We now know enough about the origins of religion in both
the human race and in individual humans to understand
that the hard-headed skepticism of the agnostic rationalist
does not provide adequate explanation for the data. Religion is rooted in experience. Humankind encounters the
sacred in a wide range of experiences, running from mystical
ecstasy to the much less dramatic experience of contingency
and limitation that contemporary writers call "limit-experiences" or "horizon-experiences." Spectacularly or mat-
ter-of-factly, humankind bumps up against the limitations
of its own existence, and in that moment of encountering
limit, it also encounters giftedness, gratuitousness, grace.
The smile of a child, the rising of the sun in the morning,

the crash of a wave, the sound of a symphony, the scent of a flower suggest to the human that there is "something more." It is in this encounter with the possibility of "more" that religion is born. That "more," whatever it may be, is the holy, the sacred, that which some of us call God.

Virtually everything else in our lives is shaped by the experience of the "more." If we perceive the "more" to be benign and gracious, then the world is defined by us as pleasant, and we adjust our lives accordingly. If we perceive the "other," the "more," as malign, difficult, contentious, or unpredictable, so, too, the universe will be defined, and we live our lives accordingly. Voltaire had it all wrong. Humankind creates its world in the image and likeness of the God it has experienced.

There are a number of primordial experiences of the sacred which seem to exist in virtually all the religions of the world. Whether they are part of a "collective unconsciousness," as Carl Jung has said, or responses to the universal structures of human existence, as Mircea Eliade argues (more plausibly, it seems to me) need not detain us. Certain phenomena seem to be everywhere at all times that are especially predisposed to bringing us into contact with "more." They are, in other words, the most likely to trigger horizon-experiences for us. Water, the sun, the moon, the tree, human sexuality, the rebirth of nature at springtime are the universal human symbols in the sense that they seem especially constructed to give us hints of what lies beyond the horizon.

Long before we have any recorded history, humankind began to put these symbols into rituals. Dances, ceremonies, stories, songs, the tracings of figures and shapes on cave walls served many purposes. They united the celebrants with the primal forces that were revealing themselves in the symbols. They guaranteed that the forces would continue to be gracious to the members of the tribe, they were a way of passing on the as yet unselfconscious beliefs of the people from generation to generation. But most important of all, they were ways of continuing the experience. Those who created the rituals had experienced the sacred through encounter with one of the archetypical phenomenon. The ritual was an overflow of that experience by which they attempted to share it with others. If you commit yourself to the ritual, in other words, you can have the same experience as did those ancient ancestors who first encountered the "other," the "more."

For our purposes it cannot be emphasized too strongly that this is what religion is all about in its essence. It is an encounter with the sacred, either a primary encounter by those religious founders who began a ritual tradition or a secondary encounter in which the ritual triggers in the followers of a tradition an experience similar to that which the founders had. Religion is rooted in experience; ritual is an attempt to reenkindle that experience. Religion is an encounter with the "Other," the "More," with what is beyond the horizon, with the sacred, the holy, the mysterious, the wonderful, with That Which Is. Ritual is a means by which the primal religious experiences are handed down from generation to generation not by formulations of doctrine but by reenkindling the experience of the founders.

Theology comes much later.

The pre-Sinai Semitic spring rituals of the Paschal Lamb and the Unleavened Bread were at some point combined, perhaps not self-consciously, into the Feast of Exodus, of Yahweh's liberation of his people, of the beginning of the new life of the Children of Israel. The feast was celebrated long before accounts of it were written down in books that came to be the Scriptures. It was only after hundreds of years of development of the Exodus tradition that more or less formal theological reflection on it would begin. Passover recalls the experience of liberation for the Children of Israel many, many centuries before their scholars and scribes got around to defining precisely what that liberation was all about. Similarly, the early Christians preached Jesus crucified and risen, the savior sent from God to free us, the new Moses leading us on a new Exodus, the new Adam presiding over the beginning of a new humanity long, long before theologians assembled in ecumenical councils to try to define precisely who and what Jesus was. Indeed, even those early prototheologians who described Jesus as the new Moses and the new Adam had already begun to reflect on an experience which in its raw, primal state could only be described in the words, "He is risen." The encounter with the risen Jesus, in other words, came many years before even the most elementary theological reflection on its meaning.

Such an approach to religion seems strange to us highly intellectualized moderns who think that ideas come before symbols and experience, and who believe that religious doctrines (usually defined solemnly by ecumenical councils) precede rituals and symbols. In fact, of course, when we stop to think about it historically it appears to be the other way around. Most of our ancestors got by with very little in the way of formal doctrine. The ceremonies, the mass, the sacraments, the stained-glass windows, the sacramentals, the churches themselves were enough to convey to them the fundamental insight of Christianity. Formal doctrine they did not know and did not need to know.

Things are more complicated today. Experience must dialogue with reflection, and formal religious thought, whether we call it "theology" or not, is essential for most of us. We must, as Paul Ricoeur puts it, "unpack" the symbol; we must analyze the experience, take it apart and figure out what it means. Then we can put it back together again and live by it, as our ancestors did.

But we should note carefully what happens when we "unpack" a symbol, analyze an experience. We do not simply find in the symbol a question which may be answered through a scientific experiment, discursive reasoning, or tortuous intellectual wrestling. The answer is already in the symbol; the limit-experience poses both the question—our own contingency—and the answer—giftedness, gratuity.

The rite of spring, particularly the Christian rite we call Easter, does not so much raise the question of human survival as it simultaneously raises it and provides the answer frequently by denying that the question we bring to the experience is the proper one. We come to the spring experience, for example, with such questions as "Is the human soul immortal?" "Is there life after death?" We find that the experience almost brushes aside such questions. As G. K. Chesterton said of his insight gleaned from the intense experience of an escape from almost certain sudden death, "Life is too important ever to be anything but life." The Christian spring festival tells us in its raw, elemental resonance that life is too strong for death. Anyone who has permitted himself to experience the full intensity of the Easter event knows that the question is no longer life *after* death but rather death *and* life, life *and* death. What is the relationship between the two? So intimately linked are they that "nothing lives but something dies, nothing dies but something lives." Of what sort is that intimate link? And in the person of the Crucified One who has risen, the Christian intuits in his spring festival that however death and life are linked, "they are twain yet one, and Death is Birth."

In a very real sense we could stop now. The Christian answer to the question of life after death is simply "Easter." It is the Christian Passover, the Christian rite of spring. Instead of perusing the rest of these pages the reader might just as well dig out a recording of the *Exsultet* and permit himself to be carried away by its rich and powerful symbolism. There is nothing much more that can be said.

Rejoice, heavenly powers! Sing, choirs of angels!
    Exult, all creation around God's throne!
    Jesus Christ, our King, is risen!
    Sound the trumpet of salvation!

Rejoice, O earth, in shining splendor,
    radiant in the brightness of your King!
    Christ has conquered! Glory fills you!
    Darkness vanishes forever!

Rejoice, O Mother Church! Exult in glory!
    The risen Savior shines upon you!
    Let this place resound with joy,
    echoing the mighty song of all God's people!

    It is truly right
    that with full hearts and minds and voices
    we should praise the unseen God, the all-powerful
        Father,
    and his only Son, our Lord Jesus Christ.

    For Christ has ransomed us with his blood,
        and paid for us the price of Adam's sin
        to our eternal Father!

This is our passover feast,
    when Christ, the true Lamb, is slain,
    whose blood consecrates the homes of all believers.

This is the night when first you saved our fathers:
    you freed the people of Israel from their slavery
    and led them dry-shod through the sea.

This is the night when the pillar of fire
    destroyed the darkness of sin!

This is the night when Christians everywhere,
    washed clean of sin
    and freed from all defilement,
    are restored to grace and grow together in holiness.

This is the night when Jesus Christ
    broke the chains of death
    and rose triumphant from the grave.

What good would life have been to us,
    had Christ not come as our Redeemer?

Father, how wonderful your care for us!
    how boundless your merciful love!
    To ransom a slave
    You gave away your Son.

O happy fault, O necessary sin of Adam,
    which gained for us so great a Redeemer!

Most blessed of all night, chosen by God
    to see Christ rising from the dead!

Of this night scripture says:
    'The night will be as clear as day;
    it will become my light, my joy.'

The power of this holy night
    dispels all evil, washes guilt away,
    restores lost innocence, brings mourners joy;
    it casts out hatred, brings us peace, and humbles
        earthly pride.

Night truly blessed when heaven is wedded to earth
  and man is reconciled with God!

Therefore, heavenly Father, in the joy of this night,
  receive our evening sacrifice of praise,
  your Church's solemn offering.

Accept this Easter candle,
  a flame divided but undimmed,
  a pillar of fire that glows to the honor of God.

Let it mingle with the lights of heaven
  and continue bravely burning
  to dispel the darkness of this night!

May the Morning Star which never sets find this
  flame still burning:
Christ, that Morning Star, who came back from the
  dead
and shed his peaceful light on all mankind,
  your Son who lives and reigns for ever and
  ever.

Amen.

In the final analysis one either buys the *"O felix culpa"* of the *Exsultet* and the "Death is Birth" of Francis Thompson or one does not. One permits oneself the spring-Easter experience and believes that it is revelatory, indeed the sacrament par excellence, or one dismisses the experience as an absurd self-deception. In either case, no argument is really possible. Neither is there any point in trying to argue with someone who refuses to run the risk of permitting himself the spring experience. If you will not sing the *Exsultet* or the *Victimae Paschali,* if you will not give the words and the music a chance to stir you out of your complacency and bring you up against the horizons of your own existence, then there is no way I or anyone else can persuade you that

what is revealed in the Easter experience is indeed the Way
Things Really Are.

But for a number of reasons it is necessary to go beyond
the experience the first Christians had of the risen Jesus
and the ritual which makes it possible for us to share that
experience. The critical modern mind must know more. It
must be able to persuade those who will not accept the insight contained in its symbols that it is not irrational or in-
human to commit oneself to symbols like the Christian
Passover. It must reassure its own hyperrational anxieties by
buttressing experience with argumentation. It must persuade or try to persuade both others and itself that if there
is no "scientific" certainty about religious truth, there is at
least converging probabilities in the arguments that suggest that That Which Is Experienced may well be That
Which Really Is.

I shall therefore leave experience and turn toward discursive argumentation, bringing evidence from a number of
different disciplines and a number of different points of
view to suggest that the conviction of life after death is not
irrational (which, as I have said before, is a bad way of
stating the Christian belief that "life is too important to be
anything but life," or "For they are twain yet one, and
Death is Birth"). But religious truth is plagued by a different kind of language and knowledge than scientific or
mathematical truth. Of its very nature religion does not
admit of empirical verification. Religion deals with that
which is ultimate, that which is "other," "more"; and of its
very essence, that which is "beyond" cannot be constrained
within the limits of operationalized variables. Any religious
truth which was empirically verifiable would no longer be
religious truth by that very fact. (Although, as we shall see

subsequently, some writers today think that it may well be possible to verify human survival. I think they are barking up the wrong tree, but that's another matter.)

Religion is grounded in experience, indeed in the most intense kinds of experiences; and it is that very intensity which precludes its verification by the methods of empirical science. A major breakthrough in contemporary religious thought occurred when people were able to distinguish between the "experiential" and the "empirical." One can and does indeed experience the "Other" in the various limit-experiences of human life, but the "Other," since it is totally other, absolutely other, cannot be empirically measured or verified.

There are principles of "validation" in religious language, but we can leave them aside for the purposes of this book.[1] These rules only establish that we are playing the religious word game properly, and that the religious symbols we use are being validly used as symbols. They cannot tell us that that which we encounter (or Whom) in limit-experiences is indeed the Way Things Really Are. Empirical methods or discursive reasoning has nothing to say one way or the other on that score—save, perhaps, for establishing that it is not completely irrational to trust that which seems to be revealed to us in the limit-experience. Once again, by definition, the judgment we make on that which has been experienced is an absolutely free decision of the personality. Religious assent cannot be constrained either by deductive argument or by empirical verification (much less by law or force, as some of our predecessors in the days of the Inquisition seemed to think). Religious assent requires not merely the intellect but the whole personality. It comes from embracing that which is revealed or, if one wishes, the

One who reveals Himself in the experience. To put the
matter differently, a limit-experience generates its own validation. By its very nature and by definition, no other validation can be found.

To put it more concretely, one can experience the triumph of life over death in spring (costly and violent, as it
is). One can experience the death and resurrection of Jesus
in the Christian Passover, but one can accept the model by
which to live the resurrection experience only when one
freely chooses to do so. One cannot be constrained to it by
rational argument. Indeed if there were rational arguments
that forced assent to the Easter mystery ("mystery" here
means "mysterion," sacrament, or revelation), then it would
cease to be a mystery and become commonplace fact. I can
establish by argument, I think, that it is not irrational to
accept the resurrection as a model by which to live. Indeed,
I think I can establish that it is even a not implausible
model. Furthermore, I can show that it is neither irrational
nor implausible to live by such a model. As Jacques Choron
wisely puts it, "It seems that one cannot extricate oneself
from the difficulties in the continuous interplay of arguments *pro* and *contra*." The best Choron can do, as we
shall see in the next chapter is to "find some measure of
reassurance against the nagging doubts of meaninglessness."
And that is as far as rational argument can go. One must
then leap one way or the other, which is to say, that one
selects those experiences in life which seem to be most revelatory and lives by them.

In his book *The Challenge of Jesus*, my friend and colleague, John Shea, points out how the tree (another one of
the primordial archetypes) triggered an experience of mean-
ingfulness in Avery Dulles that led him to Catholicism and

the priesthood. But a tree also triggered an experience of nausea and disgust in Jean Paul Sartre which drove him from the Church into existentialist atheism. One must choose between meaning and absurdity; it is a choice for which the data are necessarily and by definition inconclusive, and for which the best arguments can only provide some measure of reassurance. The choice is free.

I proceed to my rational arguments with the caveat that ultimately the reader (and the writer) must fall back upon his own experiences. We live in a time after the beginning of the celebration of the Christian Passover, and we must ask ourselves ultimately whether that which we experience or can experience in the Christian spring festival does reveal the "form in the void" (Lyall Watson's phrase). Does it reveal that there is, as Father Teilhard has put it, "something afoot in the universe, something like gestation and birth?" Is there Someone out there?

Exsultet nam angelica turba coelorum!

Chapter 3

SO LITTLE TIME

IN THE SEEMINGLY ENDLESS PAGES OF THE MANIC, COMPUL-
sive, undisciplined novel, *Fear of Flying*, Erica Jong has one
brilliant passage: "Maybe," she says, "people should only
get married when they are middle-aged. Then they'll take
care of each other because they'll know they're going to die
anyhow."

The week I read that line there was an article in the
Village Voice about "husband dumping." The same Manhattan smart set about which Ms. Jong writes has progressed
from articles describing their divorces to articles describing
the dubious and mixed blessings of life after the divorce.
The *Village Voice* piece was a sad and pathetic tale of
feminist chic. The author and her friends had made all the
stops—paperback books on open marriage, consciousness-
raising, human potential sessions, extramarital affairs, divorce, one-night stands, and now loneliness and frustration.
Somehow it hadn't turned out nearly so well as they thought
it would when they became "liberated." They were educated enough, alas, to know all about the current movement
and its ideology, but they weren't educated enough to be
skeptical about the salvation which the movement promised. Like many other half educated people in our society,
they had read themselves and verbalized themselves into a
last state worse than the first. Gail Sheehey, the author of
the article concluded with the melancholy thought that

perhaps marriage wasn't so bad after all. She just might possibly try it again.

But in the midst of her tale, there is a revelatory line: "The human potential movement forces one to think seriously about death." It is precisely the concern about death stirred up by human potential that causes a woman to wake up in the morning, look at her balding husband and say, "My God, is this all there is to life?"

Now as anyone knows who has had any dealings with the human potential people, the last thing that is on their minds is death. One can search through all the literature, listen to all the talk, absorb all the ideology, and never once hear the word "death" mentioned. Yet the author of the *Village Voice* article offers the passing, matter-of-fact comment that the human potential movement is about death. She's quite right, of course, though as far as I know she is the first one to have said it. You can avoid thinking about death if you don't become very self-conscious about your own personal development; but begin to think in life-cycle terms, begin to be concerned about personal growth, begin to worry about self-fulfillment, and the thought of death lurking around the corner is inescapable. Manhattan Island's smart set had no notion that an intellectual fashion which taught to think in terms of personal growth and life-cycle would begin to make them think about death. But once we know about the "turning thirty life crisis," the "crisis of the middle years," and the "crisis of maturity" (not forgetting, of course, the already assimilated "identity crisis" of late adolescence and the "intimacy crisis" of youth), there is no way to avoid thinking about the ultimate "crisis of death." So Gail Sheehy, Erica Jong, and *New York* magazine's radical, liberated feminist readers find themselves asking the ultimate religious question, "Is this all there is?"

Humankind, of course, is the only species that asks the question, and in the very asking there *may* be an answer. Could the universe have produced a creature that hungers desperately for permanent existence and frustrate that hunger? If it has, it is an evil universe—a possibility not to be excluded. Dylan Thomas put it nicely: "Do not go gentle into that good night./ Rage, rage against the dying of the light."

As one of the grimmest commentators on death, Edwin F. Shneideman, observes in his *Death of Man* (Quadrangle): "We must face the fact that death is the one act in which man is forced to engage. The word 'forced' has a special meaning here. It implies that death, like torture, rape, capital punishment, kidnap, lobotomy, and other degredation ceremonies is a form of coercion and impressment. The threat of being erased, of being reduced to nothingness can be viewed reasonably only as the most perfidious of forced punishment."

If that's all it is, if all the struggles, joys, hopes, disappointments, frustrations, sacrifices, plans, the expectations that constitute human life are for nothing, if truly that is all there is, then life is a tale told by an idiot, "full of sound and fury, signifying nothing," as Macbeth would have it. It is an eminently plausible interpretation, and, like Dylan Thomas, one certainly ought to rage against the dumb and vicious cosmos which has produced us only to destroy us. The existentialist argues that we should live in such a way that we don't deserve the punishment and the absurdity of our existence. But why the hell live that way? Wouldn't it be far better to live in such a way that we richly deserved

the punishment? If we do not have faith, might we not, as
G. K. Chesterton said of Higgins, at least have the fun?

> If I had been a Heathen,
>   I'd have praised the purple vine,
> My slaves would dig the vineyards,
>   And I would drink the wine;
> But Higgins is a Heathen,
>   And his slaves grow lean and grey,
> That he may drink some tepid milk
>   Exactly twice a day.
>
> If I had been a Heathen,
>   I'd have crowned Neæra's curls,
> And filled my life with love affairs,
>   My house with dancing girls;
> But Higgins is a Heathen,
>   And to lecture rooms is forced,
> Where his aunts, who are not married,
>   Demand to be divorced.
>
> If I had been a Heathen,
>   I'd have sent my armies forth,
> And dragged behind my chariots
>   The Chieftains of the North.
> But Higgins is a Heathen,
>   And he drives the dreary quill,
> To lend the poor that funny cash
>   That makes them poorer still.
>
> If I had been a Heathen,
>   I'd have piled my pyre on high,
> And in a great red whirlwind
>   Gone roaring to the sky.
> But Higgins is a Heathen
>   And a richer man than I;
> And they put him in an oven
>   Just as if he were a pie.

Now who that runs can read it,
  The riddle that I write,
Of why this poor old sinner,
  Should sin without delight—
But I, I cannot read it
  (Although I run and run),
Of them that do not have the faith,
  And will not have the fun.

"The Song of the Strange Ascetic"
G. K. Chesterton[1]

The hypothesis of absurdity is plausible, then. Life may well be, as Ernest Nagel has said, "an episode between two oblivions." Still, there is something in us that revolts against such an explanation. One of my social scientific colleagues told me of being at a dinner and seated next to a young rabbi. Since clergy-baiting was part of this good Florentine gentleman's stock in trade, he began with the innocuous comment that life did not need to have any meaning beyond itself. The rabbi agreed, as many modern rabbis are wont to do. There was no meaning in life beyond the fact of life itself. My colleague was horrified. It was all right for an agnostic social scientist to contend that there was no ultimate meaning, but, damn it to hell (one should excuse the expression), what point was there in having clergy at all if they didn't argue the opposite position? And so my colleague found himself willy-nilly arguing throughout dinner that there was indeed some purpose in life that went beyond the limits of life itself. There was, in other words, "more," and the "more" just might possibly be an "Other."

I asked him if he had won the argument. "Of course," he responded, "and now I'm trying to figure out what to do about it." It has been years since that incident, but the last letter I got from him at Christmastime ended, "May the Lord bring you peace and joy in this his season."

There is, in other words, a powerful, "instinctive" human impulse to deny the absurdity of things and to assert the purposefulness of life. But what is that purpose? That's hard to say and even harder to explain. And so the dialogue goes on in the modern mind when it thinks about death. The whole thing is either absurd or it is not; but it is absurd to say that it is absurd, and if that's true, then what is it?

This dialogue is no monopoly of modern man. It is as old as humankind. It may, however, be somewhat more poignant now because we are caught up in the dilemma of scientism and cannot admit the existence of any other kind of knowledge besides the empirically verifiable. Of course, when we deal with purpose or absurdity we are far beyond the realm of verification.

The purpose-absurdity dilemma is nowhere better described than in the last forty pages of Jacques Choron's *Death and Modern Man*. Choron, himself a modern man, bounces back and forth on the horns of the dilemma with a sharpness and honesty and clarity that is usually not to be found in the debate. He quotes the ancient French folk rhyme:

> Life is vain: a little love
> A little hate, and then good day.
> Life is short: a little hope,
> A little dream and then good night.[2]

Can that be all there is?
And Renan asks the same question:

I find death loathsome, hateful, and senseless when it

extends its coldly blind hand toward virtue and genius.
A voice tells us unceasingly: truth and goodness are
the aims of your life; sacrifice everything else to these
goals; but when we arrive toward the end of our journey
where we should have found our reward . . . this
philosophy, which promised us the secret of death,
excuses itself with an embarrassed stammer.[3]

Death, says Choron, is an obvious event, so obvious and
unequivocal that it is virtually impossible to resist the in-
ference that with the last breath all is indeed ended and that
the living, thinking, and feeling person we knew has been
irrevocably annihilated. And the impact of the spectacle of
death would be even stronger if we, as we normally do not,
observed the decomposition of the corpse.

How can we doubt, Choron asks, "that life is but a
physical and chemical process, that consciousness is but an
'epiphenomenon,' that the real man *is* his body, with the
disintegration of which the conscious personality ends?"
Choron quotes with sympathetic approval Joseph Wood
Krutch, "Living is only a physiological process with only a
physiological meaning."

Yet Choron observes that such a conclusion is totally
unacceptable to many people. He quotes the British philosopher F. C. S. Schiller:

One need not necessarily be violently enamored of
one's own life, or cherish any abject desire for personal
continuance, in order to feel that if the chapter of life
is definitely closed by death, despair is the end of all its
glories. For to assert that death is the end of all beings
is to renounce the ideal of happiness, to admit that
adaptation is impossible, and that the end of effort
must be failure. And it is to poison the whole life with

this bitter consciousness, and further, it is finally to renounce the faith in the rationality of things, which could hardly be reasserted against so wanton a waste of energy as would be involved in the destruction of characters it required so much patient toil and effort to acquire. A good and wise man dies, and his goodness and his wisdom, his incalculable powers to shape the course of things for good, are wasted and destroyed.[4]

". . . So wanton a waste of energy . . ." surely an impressive phrase. Is it all just a wanton waste of energy? If so, then indeed let us "rage, rage against the failing of the light."

And then Choron swings to the other horn of his dilemma and quotes Bertrand Russell:

. . . That man is the product of causes which had no prevision of the end they were achieving; that his origin, his growth, his hopes and fears, his loves and his beliefs, are but the outcome of accidental collocations of atoms; that no fire, no heroism, no intensity of thought and feeling, can preserve an individual life beyond the grave; that all the labor of the ages, all the devotion, all the inspiration, all the noonday brightness of human genius is destined to extinction in the vast death of the solar system, and that the whole temple of Man's achievement must inevitably be buried beneath the debris of a universe in ruins—all these things, if not quite beyond dispute, are yet so nearly certain, that no philosophy which rejects them can hope to stand.[5]

And Tolstoy makes the point more succinctly in *Anna Karenina:* "In infinite time, in infinite matter, in infinite space is formed a bubble-organism, and that bubble lasts a while and bursts; and that bubble is Me."

Choron concludes his dialectic with a marvelous Gallic shrug of the shoulders: "The world appears as a 'mixture' of the purposeless and purposeful." We cannot discover whether there is any meaning in human existence, but it does not necessarily follow that there is no meaning: "Man may not be the aim and goal of the universe, but that nature has, after all, produced self-conscious persons with their intelligence and their quest for truth, beauty, and goodness would seem to indicate strongly that this could not have been done by a universe blind to values and devoid of purpose."

Is there meaning or is there not? Choron isn't sure but he ends with "some measure of reassurance":

> For myself, I find some measure of reassurance against the nagging doubt of meaninglessness in the implications of what has been considered by some thinkers as the profoundest, even though unanswerable, question: Why is there something rather than nothing? What this question implies is that there is no necessity of there being a world at all. But precisely because it would have been so easy not to have been, the existence of the world and of my own individual self must have a significance, a meaning that goes beyond the mere fact of its and my own existing, a meaning that cannot be annulled by the fact that this existence is finite and will end, even though man might see only his mortality and be led by it to the conclusion that his existence is meaningless, he may hopefully apply to himself the words of Shakespeare: 'The summer's flower is to the summer sweet/ Though to itself, it only live and die.'

And in response to the question, "Is this all?" I would say, "How come there is even this?"

We are dealing here with hope, the unshakable and un-forfeitable conviction that there is meaning in human life (to use Schubert Ogden's phrase). The unconscious, Freud tells us, is convinced of its own immortality. Our dreams take for granted that we do not die ultimately. Hope is built into the structure of our personalities. No matter how hard we try not to hope, hope persists. When we deny it explicitly, hope is still there implicitly. Choron notes that the dying Rabelais said, "I go to look for a great perhaps." Darwin observed, "Every man must judge for himself between conflicting vague possibilities." Victor Hugo, much more confidently said to someone who thought death was the end of everything, "For your soul this may be so; as to mine, I know her to be eternal." And Maeterlinck commented, ". . . in these questions concerning life and death our imagination has remained rather rudimentary. It asks impossible things because they are too modest." And Max Scheler, that strange, haunted philosopher-sociologist-some-time Catholic, who was one of the great geniuses of the twentieth century, captures as powerfully as anyone ever has the nature of hope:

> . . . The question of survival can be decided at one point only: in the precise and clear insight into the manner of how and what we experience daily and hourly, even from second to second. . . . Do I not see, become aware and grasp directly that I am a Being, which is the master of his body, the ruler and king in the desert of dead 'things?' . . . Do I not see, grasp and perceive in each of my brethren a person as a center of a whole world, which lies beyond a few shreds of sense-perception that fall now into my eye and hand—a something that extends in depth, which my love and understanding is

never and will never be large enough to fathom; how should this my brother then not be able to outlast what is called death?[6]

At the end of her description of the five stages of preparing for death, Elizabeth Kubler-Ross discusses hope, which she sees not so much a stage in preparation as a quality that may or may not run throughout the whole experience of dying:

> In listening to our terminally ill patients we were always impressed that even the most accepting, the most realistic patients left the possibility open for some cure . . . It is this glimpse of hope which maintains them through days, weeks, or months of suffering. It is the feeling that all this must have some meaning, will pay off eventually if they can only endure it for a little while longer. . . . It gives the terminally ill a sense of a special mission in life which helps them maintain their spirits, will enable them to endure more tests when everything becomes such a strain—in a sense it is a rationalization for their suffering at times. . . . No matter what we call it, we found that all our patients maintained a little bit of it and were nourished by it in especially difficult times.[7]

In more recent research, Kubler-Ross has studied those who have "come back from the dead," that is to say, those who have been pronounced dead medically and then resuscitated. In a press interview after the preliminary report of her research, Dr. Kubler-Ross said:

> Death is a feeling of peace and hope. . . . Not one of them has ever been afraid to die again. . . . They can describe in minute detail what the experience was . . . how they float out of their bodies. . . . They have a

feeling of peace and wholeness, a tremendous feeling of 'stop all this attempt to revive me, I'm all right'—a perfectly good feeling.

The most common denominator of all these people is that when they come back, many of them resented our desperate attempts to bring them back to life.

Kubler-Ross' respondents may have been medically dead, but they were not in fact dead since they were resuscitated. What they have described is not what happens after death but what the final moment of life or the transitional moment between life and death is like. Their experience may only be an evolutionary adaptation by which a species, able to reflect on its own death, learns to die easily. It does not necessarily *prove* anything.

Many of us will be forgiven, though, for thinking that it is a very strong hint.

Hope against hope, beyond hope, when there is no hope. One hopes because one must hope; one hopes because it is implanted into the very fibers of our being, into the very center of our personalities, into every cell of the physical and psychical composite that is us. We are born with two incurable diseases: Life—always fatal—and hope—never curable. The critical question is whether hope is revelation or deception. Can we trust this extraordinarily powerful human urge? If we did not have hope, we would not even ask the question of survival. Hope forces us to ask the question, and hope implies the answer. But dare we believe it? The data are not conclusive and never can be. We have Darwin's "vague possibilities," Rabelais' "great perhaps," Graham Greene's "hint of an explanation," and Peter Berger's "rumor of angels." That's all we'll ever have. Again, you pays your money and you takes your choice.

There are, of course, those who will neither pay nor choose: The agnostics, who live on the existential fence as mugwumps (with their "mugs" on one side and their "wumps" on the other), refuse to answer at all; and the "half-an-answer-is-better-than-noners" see meaning in life but no survival after death.

It is possible to be an agnostic for a generation, I think (particularly if your father was a Protestant minister). But the lesson of history is that agnosticism is not a durable compromise. One either has the faith or the fun; one is either a believing puritan or an unbelieving pagan. Agnosticism as a compromise between faith and unbelief may be tenable philosophically but it is untenable humanly. Most agnostics choose to live as though life has a purpose and become respectable, responsible members of the upper middle class. I do not know whether I should believe an agnostic's principles of unbelief or his practice of belief, although I should be perfectly prepared to testify on his behalf if called upon to do so before the Great Judge. The agnostic's life is frequently more admirable than those who profess to believe.

The other kind of compromise goes beyond agnosticism and asserts that there is indeed purpose and meaning in life, but there need be no personal survival after death. This argument has been associated with the process philosophers and theologians, Whitehead, Harthshorne, and Ogden; with a group of scholars who write for the journal *Zygon*, and a very considerable number of Jews, who in this respect are surely pre-Pharisaic in outlook.[8]

Writers like Charles Harthshorne and Schubert Ogden are particularly strong on the subject. It is, they argue, the height of selfishness to be concerned about one's own personal survival. One should be content with the realization that one will be absorbed into the "consequential nature of God" (a process philosophy category roughly equivalent to Teilhard's Omega Point). It should not be necessary to add that one's own puny little identity does not survive such absorption.

Baloney! Either I survive, the I that I am, or the whole thing is a bad joke. What sort of a God would it be who would absorb us into Himself and snuff out our own individuality in the process? This is not exactly the gentle fellow pilgrim of whom Whitehead writes so feelingly. Process thinkers are not true to their own best instincts, I fear, in this matter. Life either has meaning for me, for my own personal speck of cosmic dust existence, or it has no meaning at all. I'm sorry, but if there is a God and He loves me, and if He is able to see to it that I survive (and for God that should be no problem) and He doesn't do it, then He is Bergman's spider after all.

Which He isn't, as the Lord Jesus has told us, and as Bergman himself knows in his better moments.

It may well be that in an earlier stage of human history, when human self-consciousness was not as highly developed as it is in our time, the question of personal human survival was not so acutely felt or asked as it is today. It is surely the case, however, that virtually all religions that we know take it for granted that the human personality survives. Even our Neanderthal predecessors (if they were not our ancestors) had funeral practices which showed they believed in the survival of the human person, however dimly they may have been able to articulate what either "survival" or "person" was. (Some archaeologists argue that the Neanderthals had very limited vocal capabilities, which may be why *homo sapiens,* as we are redundantly known, were so easily to replace—if not obliterate in the first genocide—the Neanderthals.) Even the Hebrew religion, rebelling as it did against the funeral cults of the religious world around it and insisting on moral behavior in this world, nonetheless postulated some kind of vague survival in the shadowy netherworld of "sheol."[9]

The Rig Veda of ancient India describes Mother Earth warmly receiving the body of the dead person:

> Betake thee to the lap of the earth the mother, of earth
>   far-spreading, very kind and gracious.
> Young dame, wool-soft unto the guerdon-giver, may
>   she preserve thee from Destruction's bosom.
> Heave thyself, Earth, nor press thee downward
>   heavily: afford him easy access, gently tending him.
> Earth, as a mother wraps her skirt about her child,
>   so cover him.
> Now let the heaving earth be free from motion: yea,
>   let a thousand clods remain above him.
> Be they to him a home distilling fatness, here let
>   them ever be his place of refuge.[10]

The Rig Veda does not speculate about what happens after such a warm reception. In fact, the official who presides over the funeral seems rather happy to get away from the body as quickly as he could. In the Iranian religion the nature of the welcome is much more precisely described:

> And all the gods and Amahraspands come to greet
> him and ask him how he has fared, saying, 'How was
> thy passage from those transient, fearful worlds where
> there is much evil to those worlds which do not pass

away and in which there is no adversary, O young man whose thoughts and words, deeds and religion are good?'

Then Ohrmazd, the Lord, speaks, saying, 'Do not ask him how he has fared, for he has been separated from his beloved body and has travelled on a fearsome road.' And they served him with the sweetest of all foods even with the butter of early spring so that his soul may take its ease after the three nights terror on the Bridge inflicted on him by Astvihat and the other demons, and he is sat upon a throne everywhere bejewelled. . . . And for ever and ever he dwells with the spiritual gods in all bliss for evermore.[11]

All the way around the world and two thousand years later, the Thompson River tribes in British Columbia envisaged a similar paradise:

At the end of the trail is a great lodge, mound-like in form, with doors at the eastern and the western sides, and with a double row of fires extending through it. When the deceased friends of a person expect his soul to arrive, they assemble here and talk about his death. As the deceased reaches the entrance, he hears people on the other side talking, laughing, singing, and beating drums. Some stand at the door to welcome him and call his name. On entering, a wide country of diversified aspect spreads out before him. There is a sweet smell of flowers and an abundance of grass, and all around are berry-bushes laden with ripe fruit. The air is pleasant and still, and it is always light and warm. More than half the people are dancing and singing to the accompaniment of drums. All are naked but do not seem to notice it. The people are delighted to see the newcomer, take him up on their shoulders, run around with him, and make a great noise.[12]

The relatives in Bolivia even promised adequate supplies of liquor for the afterlife:

> Finally the soul arrived at a large avenue lined with blossoming trees full of harmonious birds and knew then that it had reached the land of the Grandfather. It announced its arrival by stamping the ground with its bamboo tube. The Grandfather welcomed the soul with friendly words and washed it with a magic water which restored its youth and good looks. From then on the soul lived happily, drinking chicha and carrying on the routine activities of its former life[13]

Much more flamboyant and spectacular is the paradise of Mahayana Buddhism:

> And that world system Sukhavati, Ananda, emits many fragrant odours, it is rich in a great variety of flowers and fruits, adorned with jewel trees, which are frequented by flocks of various birds with sweet voices, which the Tathagata's miraculous power has conjured up. And these jewel trees, Ananda, have various colours, many colours, many hundreds of thousands of colours. They are variously composed of the seven precious things, in varying combinations, i.e. of gold, silver, beryl, crystal, coral, red pearls or emerald. Such jewel trees, and clusters of banana trees and rows of palm trees, all made of precious things, grow everywhere in this Buddha-field. On all sides it is surrounded with golden nets, and all round covered with lotus flowers made of all the precious things. Some of the lotus flowers are half a mile in circumference, others up to ten miles. And from each jewel lotus issue thirty-six hundred thousand kotis of rays. And at the end of each ray there issue thirty-six thousand kotis of Buddhas, with golden-coloured bodies, who bear the thirty-

two marks of the superman, and who, in all the ten
directions, go into countless world systems, and there
demonstrate Dharma.[14]

The idea of a great banquet is to be found in the Islamic
religion:

Beneath these trees are chairs and benches of light that
gleam, chairs and benches of jacinth and of jewels, and
the like of red gold, of green emerald, of musk and
ambergris, set there for the prophets, the messengers,
then for the saints and the pious, then for the martyrs
and the just, then for the Blessed from among all the
rest of the people. Over [these seats] are cloths of
brocade and satin and green silk, very precious, the silk
woven and hemmed with jacinths and with jewels, and
[on them] also are cushions of red brocade. On these
they will be given permission to seat themselves in ac-
cordance with the honourable rank each has. They will
be met by cries of welcome and applause, with ascrip-
tions of honour and merit. So each man of them will
take his station according to the measure of honour he
has with his Lord, and has position of nearness to Him
and in His favour, while the angels and the *wildan* show
them great respect in seating them. Then, when every
man has taken his place and settled himself, according
to his rank, orders will be given that they be served
with the finest food. So they will eat it and enjoy it
with such pleasure that they forget any food that they
have eaten hitherto, and everything they have ever
known before seems insignificant to them. [It will be
served to them] on platters the like of which they have
never seen before and on tables whose like they have
never beheld. Then orders will be given that they be
served the finest kinds of fruit such as they never before
have seen, and they will eat of these fruits and enjoy

thereof as much as they desire. Then orders will be
given that they be served the finest variety of drinks
such as they never yet have drunk, [served to them] in
vessels of pear and jacinth which shine brilliantly, giving out lights the like of whose splendour and loveli-
ness they have hitherto never beheld. . . .[15]

There are a number of attitudes one can assume about
such visions of life after death, some of them so simple and
some so elaborate and sophisticated. We can admire their
charm but dismiss them as irrelevant; we can assume that
those who described such paradises were excellent poets but
bad philosophers; or we can simply write them off as savages,
superstitious barbarians who are not to be taken seriously in
an age of science. That most humans in most times and in
most places have believed in life after death does not prove
that there *is* life after death. Still, only the most narrow and
rigid ethnocentric describes their testimony as irrelevant.
They were no more certain than we are, but at least they
were not ashamed to hope.

So the religions of humankind are at minimum another
piece of evidence of the universality of hope. That hope
may have been quite unspecific and collective in its view, as
in pre-Exilic Judaism, or so detailed and elaborate as to be
the center of a whole culture, as in Egyptian religion, serves
to emphasize the fact that wherever humans live or have
lived, one finds hope. Primitive or sophisticated, detailed or
generic, tentative or confident, hope is everywhere.

But in our self-conscious, self-analytic, growth-oriented,
life-cycle aware contemporary world, generic hope, vague
hope, unspecified hope, will hardly do. You cannot tell the
unhappy person that he or she has nothing to worry about
because at the end of life he will become absorbed in some

kind of great collective Unconscious, or that he will become part of the Consequent Nature of God, or that he will merge with the Omega Point. I may be nothing more than an unimportant speck of cosmic dust, but damn it all, if I don't survive, then I'm going out into that good night and raise bloody hell!

Chapter 4

SOCIOLOGY HAS ITS SAY

HOPE IS UNIVERSAL. IT MAY BE SELF-DECEPTIVE, IT MAY BE an evolutionary adaptation. Those early hominids who had stronger instincts toward hope may also have been more effective at surviving. Hope, then, may simply be the result of natural selection. Its persistence and its universality do not necessarily "prove" anything. At best, hope is a "hint of an explanation," a "rumor of angels." It is our hope, of course, that enables us to see revelation in the spring ritual and to respond enthusiastically to that revelation. Hope poses the question and offers the answer, intuitively and implicitly, long before we get around to discussing the subject and agonizing over the answer. It doesn't prove a thing, but it does almost force us to cry out that absurdity is absurd.

Hope need not explicitly conclude there is life after death. Hope is universal, primordial, and inevitable; survival after death, while asserted by all the world's religions, has been a matter about which individual humans have always been uncertain. One may wonder whether that uncertainty is greater or lesser today.

It is frequently suggested that it is. Humankind, we are told, is more skeptical than ever about the possibility of survival, because now we live in a scientific age and understand that life is essentially a physical and chemical process, and consciousness is "epiphenomenal." It is asserted that

58

the young and better educated are particularly able to dispense with the doctrine of human survival.

Even if such assertions are true, nothing follows from it necessarily. The young and the better educated might just as well be wrong as right. All change is not progress or growth. The pertinent question is not whether young people and better educated people are likely to believe in human survival, but whether humans do indeed survive. There is no particular reason to disenfranchise the old or the less well educated when it comes to voicing an opinion on the matter.

Still, because our age is strongly influenced by a pop evolutionary philosophy, it is worth asking whether there has been any change in the last forty or fifty years, let us say, in the proportion of people who believe in human survival after death. One asks the question not because religious truth is arrived at by counting noses but because pseudo-scientific fallacies and pop evolutionary philosophy can be disproved by social scientific data. The evidence to be gathered together in this chapter, I would suggest, will indicate that at least in the United States there has been little change in the last forty years in the belief in human survival; and there is no evidence that either the young or the better educated are less likely to believe in life after death. All such a non-change proves is that one does not lose one's place in the evolutionary vanguard by continuing to believe in human survival. Nor need one reject the possibility of survival on the grounds that one has to in order to keep up with the wave of history.

The survey data on attitudes toward death which I present in this chapter was collected from a number of major countries at various periods in time. The principal hy-

pothesis to be tested is the so-called "secularization theory,"
which contends that in advanced industrial societies, educated, sophisticated human beings cannot take religious
myths seriously. The more industrialized the society and
the more recent the survey indicator, it would be argued by
the secularization hypothesis, the lower will be the proportion of the population that believes in life after death.

The data summarized in Table 1 are necessarily ambiguous. The surveys were taken at different times in different
countries, with sampling frames of varying quality, in the
context of different surveys, and with question wordings
that may not convey quite the same nuances in one language that they do in another. Furthermore, it is quite possible that even if the accurate nuances were captured, there
would be political and social implications in the belief in
life after death that would differ from country to country.
Thus, in one country it may be difficult to be a member of
a left-wing political movement and concede belief in a
doctrine that has been used by the right wing to oppress or
control the working classes. One would have to get at deep-
seated religious convictions under such circumstances
through a rather different kind of question.

But with these reservations, Table 1 still provides fascinating though complex information. If one concedes that
the United States is the most advanced and most sophisticated industrial society in the world, and that the American
people have the highest educational attainment in the
world, then there is no confirmation for the secularization
hypothesis in Table 1. Belief in life after death has remained
at a high level in the United States between 1936 and 1973,
with some fluctuations up and down, but with a net gain of
3 percentage points in those asserting belief in survival.

TABLE 1

INTERNATIONAL DATA ON BELIEF IN LIFE AFTER DEATH

(Per Cent Believing)

	1936	1939	1944	1945	1947	1948	1958	1960	1961	1964	1968	1973
U.S.A.	64	—	76	—	68	68	—	74	74	—	73	70
Canada	—	—	—	84	78	—	—	—	68	—	—	—
England	—	49	—	—	49	—	—	—	56	—	38	—
Czechoslovakia	—	—	—	38	—	—	—	—	—	—	—	—
Brazil	—	—	—	—	78	—	48	—	—	—	—	—
Norway	—	—	—	—	71	—	66	—	71	—	54	—
Finland	—	—	—	—	69	—	—	—	—	—	55	—
Holland	—	—	—	—	68	—	—	—	63	—	50	—
Australia	—	—	—	—	63	—	—	—	—	—	—	—
France	—	—	—	—	58	—	—	—	57	—	—	—
Denmark	—	—	—	—	59	—	—	—	—	—	—	—
Sweden	—	—	—	—	49	—	—	—	—	—	38	—
Greece	—	—	—	—	—	—	—	—	—	—	58	—
West Germany	—	—	—	—	—	—	47	—	38	38	42	—
Switzerland	—	—	—	—	—	—	—	—	55	—	—	—
Japan	—	—	—	—	—	—	30	—	—	—	—	—

For the other countries the picture is more ambiguous. There is no major downswing between 1947 and 1961, generally speaking, save in Brazil (in a survey apparently limited to cities). But in the short seven years between 1961 and 1968, there were dramatic declines in England, Norway, and Holland, and a moderate increase in West Germany.

Even in 1968, however, in only three of the countries for which data were available—England, Sweden, and West Germany—does less than half the population believe in life after death. In contrast, in 1958, only 30 per cent of the Japanese believed in life after death.

It is difficult to say what the reason for the decline between 1961 and 1968 was. It was a period of unparalleled prosperity in Europe. Perhaps the abundance of goods led to a weakening of religious faith, or perhaps there was a change in the wording of the questions put to the respondents. In Germany, for example, the "don't know" response was replaced by an "impossible to say," which may have notably changed the options available to the respondents.

There are fascinating historical, sociological, and religious questions we might ask on the basis of Table 1. Why, for example, are citizens of one of the two great English-speaking democracies twice as likely to believe in life after death as the citizens of the other? If we grant that there has been no modification of question-wording in the last fifteen years, why has there been a general decline in Western European countries in secularization, where presumably it should be the farthest advanced? Such variation in the North Atlantic cultural community, which has so much in common in so many ways, suggests that intensive research ought to be done not merely on religious beliefs in these various countries but in the context of their basic belief systems.

The secularization hypothesis would also suggest that it is precisely among the young and among the better educated that evolution away from religious superstition ought to be most evident. Cross-tabulations by sex, denomination, age, and education were available for three countries. They are presented in Tables 2–5. In all three countries, the United States, Germany, and England, women are more likely to believe in life after death than men, though the differences in the United States (6 percentage points in 1973) were less than half as great as the differences in the two European countries.

TABLE 2

BELIEF IN LIFE AFTER DEATH BY SEX
(Per Cent)

Country and Year	Male	Female
United States		
1944	73	79
1960	68	78
1973	67	73
Germany		
1964	31	44
England		
1968	32	46

Protestants, Catholics, and "others"[1] are most likely to believe in human survival in the U. S. In Germany, Catholics are more likely to believe in survival than Protestants. Obviously these two denominational affiliations mean something very different in the two countries, although the proportion of American Catholics who believe in life after death in the 1973 National Opinion Research Center

(NORC) study seems surprisingly small. (Checked against two other NORC studies, however, the data in Table 3 seem to stand.)

TABLE 3

BELIEF IN LIFE AFTER DEATH BY DENOMINATION
(Per Cent)

Country and Year	Protestant	Catholic	Jew	None	Other
United States					
1973	71	70	31	33	73
Germany					
1964	30	49	—	—	31

Finally, Tables 4 and 5 test the secularization hypothesis. Are the young and the better educated less likely than other population groups to believe in life after death? In the United States and in Germany the relationship is curved, with those of intermediate education most likely to believe in survival. But the differences are very small—4 points in the U. S. and 6–7 points in Germany. The secularization hypothesis is not sustained in Table 4. The better educated are not inclined to be skeptical.

TABLE 4

BELIEF IN LIFE AFTER DEATH
BY EDUCATIONAL ATTAINMENT
(Per Cent)

Country and Year	Primary	Secondary	Higher
United States			
1973	68	72	68
Germany			
1964	37	44	38

Furthermore, while the very old are slightly more likely than others to believe in human survival (Table 5), there is no linear relationship between age and belief in life after death. The differences between the youngest age category and those in their sixties in the United States is 7 percentage points, in Germany, 5 percentage points, and in England, 2 percentage points. Thus there is no reason to believe that in these three countries rising levels of education or the moving of new age cohorts through the life cycle will lead to a notable decline in belief in life after death. The secularization hypothesis is *not* sustained by Table 5.

TABLE 5

BELIEF IN LIFE AFTER DEATH BY AGE

(Per Cent)

Age	United States 1973	Germany 1964	England 1968
20–29	69	34	37
30–39	69	37	35
		(30–44 yrs. old)	
40–49	69		41
50–59	69	39	35
		(45–69 yrs. old)	
60–69	73	46	41
		(Over 60) (65 and over)	
Over 70	76		

A more dramatic question than belief after death is actual contact with the dead. As far as we know, this question has been asked in only one survey, the Basic Belief study con-

ducted in the United States by NORC in 1973. A surprisingly high number of Americans—25 per cent—report that
they have been "really" in contact with the dead.[2]

Who were the people who had such experiences? As one
might expect, such experiences were more frequent with the
old. Two-fifths of those over sixty reported such experiences,
and 9 percent of those over seventy reported them "frequently" (a category combining respondent's specifying
that they have had such experiences "more than twice" and
"often"). But 31 percent of the teenagers reported such
experiences, which makes them more likely to report them
than anyone in their twenties, thirties, and forties (Table
6). Older people are most likely to have experienced bereave-
ment, so they are perhaps more likely to *want* contact with
the dead. The relatively high score among teenagers is
harder to explain—perhaps they are more psychically sensitive or simply more interested in bizarre events and more
likely to want to experience them.

Women are more likely than men to have had contact
with the dead. Blacks are much more likely to report it than
whites, with 46 percent of the black population having had
at least one such experience, and 23 percent having it
frequently.

Table 7 shows that of the three major religious affiliations,
Jews are more likely to report contact with the dead (even
though Jewish belief in an afterlife is not nearly so strong
as the Christian), and Protestants are more likely to report
it than Catholics. But even though 18 percent of those who
have no religion at all report some contact with the dead,
two-fifths of those whose religion is "other" claim such
contact. Among the Protestant denominations, the Episcopalians are most likely to have had a contact with the dead

TABLE 6

DEMOGRAPHIC BACKGROUND OF THOSE WHO HAVE CONTACT WITH THE DEAD
(Per Cent in U.S.A.)

Age			Sex			Race		
	Ever	Fre-quent-ly		Ever	Fre-quent-ly		Ever	Fre-quent-ly
Teens	31	0	Male	23	3	White	24	3
20's	23	2	Female	34	4	Black	46	5
30's	21	2						
40's	27	4						
50's	34	3						
60's	40	4						
Over 70	39	9						

experience, followed by the "other" Protestants (mostly fundamentalist denominations), and then by the Methodists. Forty-four percent of the Episcopalian respondents report at least one contact with the dead, as have 32 percent of the Methodists. The relatively low Roman Catholic score may be the result of the fact that Catholics are more likely to believe in human survival and have less need of such experiences—though as we shall see later, belief in survival correlates quite positively with contact with the dead. Among the Catholic ethnic groups, the Poles and the Spanish-speaking (34 percent each) are those who most frequently report contact with the dead experience. The Germans are the least likely among both Protestants and Catholics to report such experiences. One colleague has suggested to me that the high incidence of contact with the dead among the Poles and the Jews is the result of the fact

TABLE 7

CONTACT WITH THE DEAD EXPERIENCES BY RELIGIOUS AFFILIATION, PROTESTANT DENOMINATION, AND RELIGIO-ETHNICITY
(Per Cent in U.S.A. Ever)

Affiliation	Per Cent	Protestant Denomination	Per Cent	Religio-Ethnicity	Per Cent
Protestant (899)	30	Baptist (282)	28	Protestant	
Catholic (361)	26	Methodist (181)	32	British (167)	30
Jew (29)	32	Lutheran (101)	28	German (131)	24
Other (98)	40	Presbyterian (74)	27	Scandinavian (47)	21
None (46)	18	Episcopalian (35)	44	Irish (72)	31
		Other (173)	35	American (87)	24
		No denomination (40)	67	Catholic	
				Irish (47)	25
				German (48)	15
				Italian (52)	30
				Polish (43)	34
				Spanish-Speaking (33)	34
				Jew (28)	33

that in both groups there are very strong ties with parents, ties which may facilitate the conviction that a deceased parent has not completely ended his existence.

Contact with the dead correlates negatively with education and income (Table 8). Those who have had such experiences are less likely to have been to college and less likely to earn over $10,000 than are those who have not had such experiences.

TABLE 8

CONTACT WITH THE DEAD EXPERIENCES
BY EDUCATION AND INCOME
(Per Cent)

Frequency of Experience	College	$10,000 or more
Never	35	50
Once or twice	25	48
Several times	27	38
Often	23	22

Is there any relationship between marital status and contact with the dead? Are those who have lost a spouse likely to have such experiences? It is obvious that they are (Table 9). Half of those who have lost a spouse report "real" contact with the dead, and 12 percent report such contact "often." To look at the matter the other way round, 21 percent of those who have had contact with the dead are widows or widowers, and 28 percent who have had frequent contact with the dead are widows or widowers, but this group is only 7 percent of the population.

It could also be argued that if somehow the barrier that separates the living from the dead can be penetrated, it would most likely be accomplished by those who are still

TABLE 9

CONTACT WITH THE DEAD EXPERIENCES BY MARITAL STATUS
(Per Cent in U.S.A.)

Marital Status	Never	Frequency Once or Twice	Several Times	Often
Married (1053)	74	16	7	3
Widowed (110)*	49	18	21	12
Divorced (64)	63	27	8	3
Separated (32)	66	22	13	0
Never Married	73	16	8	2

* Twenty-one per cent of the sample who had contact with the dead "several times" and 28 per cent of the sample reporting it "often" are widowed. They are only 7 per cent of the general population.

united in a powerful bond of love. Who else, in other words, would be expected to maintain contact after death? Besides, the correlation is a correlation, not a total explanation. Those who have contact with the dead tend to be older people, women, widows and widowers. They differ from the rest of the population in only one respect: They are less well educated.

Does it not follow that those who are better educated and more sophisticated are less likely to fall victim to such superstitious nonsense? The question is a fair one, but it must be noted that levels of educational attainment have changed over the last half century, and older people are much less likely to have graduated from high school and to have gone to college. Thus the question becomes, does the lower level of educational achievement relate directly to contact with the dead experience, or is it merely a spurious relationship, resulting from the fact that older people are less well educated?

Figure 1 indicates decisively that the latter is the case. In the three-variable model there is no correlation between attending college and contact with the dead. Being over forty relates both negatively to college attendance and positively to contact with the dead, and the relationship between attending college and not having such experiences "often" or "several times" turns out to be spurious.

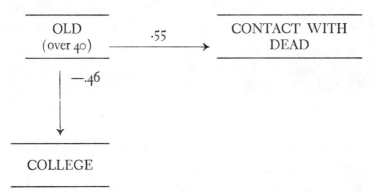

Figure 1—Relationship between Age and Education with Contact with the Dead Experiences "Often" or "Several Times."

What does it mean to say that more than half the people in the North Atlantic community believe in life after death, and that one-quarter of the people in the United States report having had actual contact with the dead? Does this represent a decline from some previous age of faith, or does it rather indicate continuity with the past? Unfortunately there is no good way to answer the question. Any attempt to postulate higher levels of belief in survival for any earlier era of Western history must necessarily be extremely speculative. We do not know how citizens of the thirteenth, the fifteenth, seventeenth, or ninth centuries would respond to

questions from a Gallup or an NORC interview. But it is
naive to think that atheism, agnosticism, skepticism, and
doubt are twentieth-century discoveries. We know, of
course, that there have been "Godless" districts in England
and France for hundreds of years. French researchers suggest that "missions" in certain districts many hundreds of
years ago have shaped the religiousness of those districts
ever since. Similarly, revivalistic movements in England of
the seventeenth and eighteenth centuries seem to account
for the considerable diversity in religious practice in different
sections of the English countryside. It is not unreasonable
to assume that there never was a time in human history
when belief in survival was easy.

So it is inappropriate to ask why the conviction of human
survival has fallen to such low levels. We might just as well
ask why it has remained at such a high level despite the
attacks of the various secularizing forces to which so much
of the literature of sociology of religion is devoted. Instead
of trying to find trends where there are no base lines, it
would seem better to be content to ask why so many people
believe in life after death.

Chapter 5

THE WONDER SCIENCES

LET US RECAPITULATE. I HAVE CONTENDED THAT BOTH THE question and the answer of human survival are found in "limit-experiences" or "horizon-experiences" in which we come against the horizons of our existence and get a vague hint that there is something beyond the horizon. There are certain experiences that are limit-experiences par excellence. Of these, the spring, the rebirth of nature, is the one that most powerfully resonates with the human longing for survival. Rituals serve to reproduce both for the founders and for subsequent generations the experiences which begin great religious traditions. Spring rituals reproduce the experience of spring as a sacrament, as a revelation of human longings and expectations. The Christian spring ritual shows that life and death are inextricably linked: "They are twain yet one, and Death is Birth." The Crucified One is risen.

Then I suggested that we speak further on the subject of human survival only to reassure ourselves that the illumination and direction which takes possession of us in the Easter ritual is not irrational or implausible. The first step in reassurance is to point out that the cause of limit-experiences is the human capacity to hope, indeed the human necessity to hope. Limit-experiences are both the cause and the effect of hope; it predisposes us to have them, indeed, makes it inevitable that we shall. The experiences, in their turn, reconfirms, revalidates, and reassures us.[1] The second step in reassurance was to use sociological data to point out that we are not alone in our conviction about human survival, that there seems little evidence of change, at least in the United States in the last half-century, of the proportion of people who believe in survival, and that the young and the better educated (presumably the "vanguard" of progress) are no different from anyone else in their willingness to believe in life after death. In this chapter I turn to a third kind of reassurance, the work of a collection of disciplines which I call, for want of a better name, the "wonder sciences." They are psychic research, parapsychology, the study of altered states of consciousness, and similar investigations. In the following chapter I will focus on one particular brand of "wonder" research, the extraordinary findings uncovered by my colleague William McCready and me in our study of the prevalence and incidence of ecstatic religious experience. Let me observe once again that it is not my intention to "prove" the fact of life after death, for, as I have pointed out before, by definition such reality cannot be constrained by the limitations of empirical validation. (Here, I think, some of the practitioners of the wonder sciences may disagree with me.) I am merely providing reassurance that our hopefulness on the subject of human survival is not irrational.

I call these disciplines "wonder sciences" specifically because the study of them forces us to keep our capacity for wonder alive, and proves to us quite powerfully that we live in an open universe that still has the capacity to surprise us.

The closed, mechanistic, unmysterious universe of the ordinary empirical sciences, or at least of the philosophers and so-called "humanists" who pontificate on the basis of what they think are the ordinary empirical sciences, simply does not stand up in the face of the wonder disciplines. Life is more than just a physical and chemical process with consciousness as an epiphenomenon.

Two qualifications are in order. Even though their findings are rejected on a priori and dogmatic grounds by many of their scientific colleagues, the wonder scientists still claim to be scientists. They are dealing with phenomena that are "marvelous" and "wonderful" in the strict sense of the words, but they would also contend that they are following the scientific method in studying phenomena which admit of scientific explanation. Their universe has more mystery than does that of Ernest Nagle, let us say, but ultimately their universe is also closed. It is simply that the closing takes place at a point far beyond that which a man like Nagle would concede.

Secondly, many of those who are actually practicing in the more traditional empirical sciences do not deny mystery. Cousteau, after floating several weeks in a submarine down the gulf stream, issued a statement filled with a sense of awe and mystery. We know more than we ever did about the gulf stream, he pointed out, but we now also know how much more we don't know. The more we know, the more mysterious the universe becomes.

Still, psychic research, parapsychology, the study of altered states of consciousness reveal a far more complex and wonderful universe than that of mere physical and chemical processes. What is more, they enable us to conclude with a high degree of confidence that there is a dimension of the human composite which is able to operate, at least for brief periods of time, independently of the human body. They also enable us to conclude, I think, that on the basis of strict empirical evidence human survival is more probable than not.[2]

Karlis Osis of the American Society for Psychical Research has a fascinating description of how death might be handled in the years to come:

> Let me make it clear by envisioning a hypothetical hospital in the year 2001. The physician is no longer so important in the hospital now. The patient is hooked up to a computer which samples his body processes constantly so that the best medication and treatment is automatically assigned to the patient. There is a single meter—the life expectancy meter—which has a rising green-colored column of fluid while the patient's chances are good. When the descending column hits that critical mark where the chance of death is almost certain, then the green color of the ink changes to the blue color of the other world.
>
> At this point, medical treatment oriented to recovery is discontinued. Orderlies in blue uniforms enter and take the patient to the Other World wing of the hospital where treatment prepares the patient for the great transition. Each will be treated according to his personality style and life history, e.g., an introvert poet differently from an extrovert plumber. The computer will select the appropriate approach, say, subroutine 21b for the poet. These treatment procedures will provide maximum opportunity for the patient to have mystical awareness of the other world. It might involve some form of counseling, inspirational passages or music, or even electrical and chemical stimulation for increased awareness. The relatives, who normally tend to be excessively mournful and disturbing to the patient, are given happiness pills and are ministered to by the chaplains. The purpose is to raise the conscious-

ness of the group of relatives and friends so that their good spiritual vibrations will create the right atmosphere for the departing soul. The chaplain will be trained to go out of the body and guide the dying patient in loosening his spirit from the entanglements of his body, and introduce him to deceased relatives on the other side. These spirits will take over and help him to follow into the next life to those regions of the spiritually advanced which he has merited. When the last breath is gone and the computer indicates the brain has almost entirely shut down, the relatives and friends will not weep but sing a glorious song of joy—bon voyage to a new existence.

This glimpse of the future has been presented partly with tongue in cheek, of course. But in all seriousness, I will predict that religious ministry to the dying in 2001 will be nearer to the futuristic fantasy I have painted here than to the obsolete last rites that the faithful now so often receive. To this end, at least decades of humble, determined, cooperative research by parapsychologists and religionists is essential. If we truly love truth more than our pet ideas, we can work together![3]

I am profoundly skeptical about the possibility of this vision ever being achieved. I do think it possible that some form of dynamism associated with the human personality does hover near the body of the deceased for a relatively brief time after death. It may be possible to communicate with it. Whether we should want to or try to do so is debatable. It may be that other spiritual dynamisms hover close by at the moment of death, although they have shown no disposition to communicate with us thus far in human history. Why they should wish to do so now, I don't understand. Nonetheless it might be possible for us to intrude upon them, but I am not sure that we should try to do so. It does seem to me that the time must come when the separation between the living and the dead is decisive. Various forms of extrasensory communication may postpone the separation, but I doubt that they can eliminate it. This is, of course, a philosophical predisposition on my part. I think the ultimates of the universe do not admit of empirical validation, and I contend this on philosophical and, probably, theological grounds. Osis and his colleagues think they might. I stand ready, as should any good scholar or, indeed, any intelligent human being, to weigh the evidence with skepticism but with an open mind. At present, I conclude that while their research seems to improve the probabilities of human survival, the evidence is anything but conclusive.

To make clear where I stand in the welter of confusing discussion about the paranormal, I believe that the extrasensory perception and psychokinesis has been proved beyond any reasonable doubt. The sort of evidence that J. B. Rhine and his colleagues have amassed through almost a half century of research could have existed on any other subject but parapsychology and have long since been accepted by the scientific community. That the existence of such phenomena is still rejected by many, indeed most, scientists is proof not that the parapsychologists are wrong but that dogmatism persists in every human institution.[4]

I also must acknowledge—somewhat to my surprise—that the burden of the evidence is such that we must admit to a high degree of probability that clairvoyance and "out of body" experiences also occur.[5] I am also persuaded that there are strange forms of communication between us and the nonhuman universe. The research evidence which shows that plants can be affected by music, by our conversation, by our thoughts about them, and even by our praying over them is remarkably persuasive. Soviet research has shown that a mother rabbit is aware of when an offspring of hers is killed in a submarine under the ocean one thousand miles away.[6]

The Kirlian photographic techniques (developed by the Russian scientist Semyon Kirlian) has discovered high frequency energy discharges from all living objects. As Kirlian says, "In living things we see the signals of the inner state of the organism reflected in brightness, dimness, and the color of the flares. The inner life activities of the human being are written in these light hieroglyphics." One of the most extraordinary Kirlian discoveries has been to take photographs of a leaf after part of it has been cut away. For a short while, the image of the removed part exists as a "ghost" on the photograph, making a complete outline of the whole original leaf.

Russian scientists conclude that there is some kind of "energy matrix" in all living things that has a shape like that of the organism but is relatively independent from it. The Russians call it the "biological plasma body."[7] One of Kirlian's associates, Michail Gaikin has found that the strongest flares in the human body correspond directly to the points on the Chinese acupuncture charts—all of which looks like some sort of Communist plot!

Some people claim to be able to see these "auras," or energy discharges, or electro-magnetic fields, or "bioplasmic bodies" (call it what you will) which emanate from the human body. Perhaps the halos in the pictures of the saints were not just artistic fantasies. In any case, McCready and I

are now preparing to try to find out what portion of the
American population claims to have actually seen such
energy discharges.[8]

Other psychic researchers have concentrated on the direct
study of evidence of human survival—out of body experience, apparitions, mediumistic phenomena, reincarnation
phenomena, and death-bed experiences. On balance they
conclude that survival is the more probable of the two
hypotheses, survival or annihilation.

C. J. Ducasse, in his monograph, "Paranormal Phenomena, Science and Life after Death,"[9] concludes his reflections
thus:

> The conclusion is . . . the same as that which was
> reached in the end by Mrs. Sidgwick, by Lord Balfour,
> by Professor Hyslop, by Dr. Hodgson, by Sir Oliver
> Lodge, and by a number of others—all of them persons
> who were thoroughly familiar with the evidence on
> record; who were gifted with keenly critical minds; who
> had originally been skeptical of the reality or even
> possibility of survival; and who were also fully ac-
> quainted with the evidence for the reality of telepathy
> and of clairvoyance, and with the claims that had been
> made for the telepathy-clairvoyance interpretation of
> the evidence, as against the survival interpretation of it.
>
> Their conclusion was essentially that the balance of
> the evidence so far obtained is on the side of the
> reality of survival and, in the best cases, of survival not
> merely of memories of the life on earth, but of survival
> also of the most significant capacities of the human
> mind, and of the continuing exercise of them after
> death.

The problem, as Ducasse implies, with much of the
evidence for contact with the dead is that once one con-

cedes the possibility of PK[10] one must admit the possibility that almost any kind of external phenomenon can be produced consciously, semiconsciously, or unconsciously by the human mind. Virtually all contact with the dead phenomena may be the simple result of parapsychological wish-fulfillment.

But perhaps not all of them. Ducasse reports one classic case where *apparently* no one alive could have had the information necessary to produce the phenomenon through some elaborate form of PK.

Another case . . . is that of the will of James L. Chaffin, a North Carolina farmer, who in November, 1905 made a will attested by two witnesses in which he left his farm to his son, Marshall, the third of his four sons, and nothing to the other three sons or to his wife. In January, 1919, however, he made a new will, not witnessed but legally valid because it was wholly in his own handwriting. In it he first stated that it was being made after his reading of the 27th chapter of Genesis; and then that he wanted his property divided equally between his four children, and that they must take care of their mother. He then placed this will at the 27th chapter of Genesis in a Bible that had belonged to his father, folding over the pages to enclose the will.

He died in 1921 without ever having mentioned to anybody the existence of the second will. The first will was not contested and was probated by its beneficiary. But some four years later the second son, James Pinkney Chaffin, began to have very vivid dreams that his father appeared to him at his bedside, without speaking. Later in June of 1925, however, the father again appeared at the bedside wearing a familiar black overcoat, and then spoke, saying "You will find my will in my overcoat pocket." The coat was eventually found in his brother's house, and examined. The inside lining of the inside pocket had been stitched together. On cutting the stitches, James found a little roll of paper on which, in his father's handwriting, were written only the words: "Read the 27th chapter of Genesis in my daddie's old Bible." James then returned to his mother's house, accompanied by his daughter, by a neighbor, and by the neighbor's daughter. When they found the Bible and opened it at the 27th chapter of Genesis, they found the second will. It was admitted to probate in December of the same year.[11]

A more distinguished personage reports a similar experience. Carl Jung, psychoanalyst, describes a peculiar experience that happened to him:

THE CARL JUNG CASE

One night I lay awake thinking of the sudden death of a friend whose funeral had taken place the day before. I was deeply concerned. Suddenly I felt that he was in the room. It seemed to me that he stood at the foot of my bed and was asking me to go with him. I did not have the feeling of an apparition; rather, it was an inner visual image of him, which I had explained to myself as a fantasy. But in all honesty I had to ask myself, 'Do I have any proof that this is a fantasy? Suppose it is not a fantasy, suppose my friend is really here and I decided he was only a fantasy— would that not be abominable of me?' Yet I had equally little proof that he stood before me as an apparition. Then I said to myself, 'Proof is neither here nor there! Instead of explaining him away as a fantasy, I might just as well give him the benefit of the doubt and for experiment's sake credit him with reality.' The moment I had that thought, he went to the door and beckoned me to follow him. So I was going to have to play along with him. That was something I hadn't bargained for. I had to repeat my argument to myself once more. Only then did I follow him in my imagination.

He led me out of the house, into the garden, out to the road, and finally to his house. (In reality it was several hundred yards away from mine.) I went in, and he conducted me into his study. He climbed on a stool and showed me the second of five books with red bindings which stood on the second shelf from the top. Then the vision broke off. I was not acquainted with his library and did not know what books he owned. Certainly I could never have made out from below the titles of the books he had pointed out to me on the second shelf from the top.

This experience seemed to me so curious that next morning I went up to his widow and asked whether I could look up something in my friend's library. Sure enough, there was a stool standing under the bookcase I had seen in my vision, and even before I came closer I could see the five books with red bindings. I stepped up on the stool so as to be able to read the titles. They were translations of the novels of Emile Zola. The title of the second volume read: *The Legacy of the Dead.* The contents seemed to me of no interest. Only the title was extremely significant in connection with this experience.[12]

The reader may judge for himself how convincing are the two incidents related here—and the scores more he can find if he digs into the paranormal literature.

What can we conclude from the wonder disciplines, from ESP, psychokinesis, out-of-body experiences, clairvoyance,

Kirlian-auras and similar phenomena? One can minimally conclude that there are forms of communication which are extrasensory, that is to say, they operate independently of the ordinary process of the impingement of energy waves on sensory nerves—at least insofar as we understand this process. It may also be possible to conclude that there is some kind of "entelechy" or "*force directrice*" which is united with the body, organizes its experiences and memories, but can to some extent operate independently of it. As Lyall Watson puts it:

> The assumption of a second system intimately associated with the normal body does provide answers for all kinds of problems that we have left hanging without solution. The organizer that produces the directional patterns of life and death . . . could be located here. Information acquired by the physical body or the somatic system could be stored as integral parts of this organizer and provide a base for memory and recall. If such a fellow traveler does exist, I think it is necessary to assume that it does have some physical reality and is not unlocated like some cosmic vapor. . . . It need not follow the shape and pattern of the body in detail, but might bear the same relationship to it that an electromagnetic field does to the conductor that lies at its center.[13]

Watson concludes:

> At this stage, all such suggestions are purely speculative. All we have established so far is that there are good reasons to presume that an alternative or supplement to our somatic system could serve a useful evolutionary purpose, and that there is nothing in biology to suggest that such a system would be impossible, or does not exist.[14]

Some evidence shows that there is a slight but immediate loss of weight at the instant of death. Perhaps, suggest some of the psychic researchers, this loss of weight represents the departure of the bioplasmic body or the organizing energy field. At death, then, the physical body dies, but the energy field survives for a time.[15] Watson is appropriately cautious: "There is no irrefutable scientific evidence for an alternative system to the familiar somatic one, but the discovery of life fields suggests that we have by no means explored all the possibilities."[16]

Out-of-body experiences, if they are not merely some form of communication that we can understand but in fact represent a departure, however temporary and partial, of the life fields and the physical body, raise some very interesting possibilities. As Watson says:

> The prevalence and consistency of out-of-body experiences suggest that separation in space may well be possible. There is nothing in biology that denies this possibility, and much that could be simply and logically explained by the existence of a relatively independent second system.
>
> We know that dissociation within the body and brain is a common occurrence, and it seems that there is no valid reason for setting spatial or temporal limits to the process. The techniques for producing detachment by conscious control create conditions that are very similar to those that occur spontaneously in anesthesia, accidental unconsciousness, and dying. If separation can take place in a living organism, and there is much to suggest that it does, we cannot deny that it could also take place in one that is in the ambivalent state that follows clinical death.
>
> So it is biologically possible for an individual, in some form and at least for a short while, to survive death.

Watson is appropriately cautious. The energy field is an interesting scientific hypothesis for which there is some evidence. There is also some evidence for out-of-body experiences. Such experiences *may* actually represent a case in which the life field can partially depart from the body and operate at some distance from it (though, even granting the existence of out-of-body experiences, other explanations are possible). Putting all these possible explanations together, one comes up with the possibility that there is some kind of dimension of the human personality which has a minute physical mass that can operate independently of the human body (at least more or less independently) under certain circumstances. If there is such a dimension to personality, it could conceivably persist after what we describe as bodily death.

Most of the possibilities listed in the previous very contingent paragraph are subject to further research. One can learn more about out-of-body experiences, one can come to understand better the mechanisms of extrasensory perception in communication, one can come to learn more about the electromagnetic forces and fields which seem to be associated with the human body. Presumably in years to come, research will clarify, refine, and verify (or falsify) those still very general hypotheses. All they will prove, however, is that there is an aspect of the human personality that can operate independently of the body, perhaps surviving for a time after the body has died. (It may even be possible to verify this possibility.)

But even if all the hypotheses listed above are supported in something like the form in which they are now stated, it will not prove life after death, much less the resurrection of Christians. It will not even refute the notion that life is a physical and chemical process. However, it would be very difficult to contend that consciousness is merely an epiphenomenon, should the hypothesis be supported. It would be even harder to deny the existence of a human "soul." On the contrary, the existence of a soul which *might* survive death could be taken to be proven. While I am skeptical of the Osis vision of the hospital for the dying at the beginning of the next century, I would not be skeptical of the possibility of a scientific demonstration of "the existence of a soul" (in Watson's sense, of course). It would be a crowning irony if the Russians beat us to it.

The existence of a human soul which might survive death at least for a time and perhaps indefinitely does not prove resurrection, but it would put on the defensive those who argue in the terms of the scientific worldview that life after death is impossible. One still would deal with a great "perhaps." But it would seem substantially less than irrational.

The wonder sciences provide reassurance. They suggest that the universe is a marvelously more complex place than we had thought, and that the rigid, mechanistic scientific worldview that we learned in our freshman philosophy courses is a much less than adequate model for the rich complexities of our universe. Such reassurance does not and cannot solve our problems definitively, but it encourages us at least that it is not irrational to trust our hopes.

In the next chapter I shall return to a form of knowledge in an altered state of consciousness which does not deal at all with probability. On the contrary, he who has had an ecstatic experience is absolutely certain of the goodness and purposefulness of the universe and of his own personal survival in it. His spectacular limit-experience leaves him with no doubts at all. He is not merely reassured, he is certain. The object of his certainty cannot be scientifically or empirically validated, of course, but that does not bother him in the least. If you have had one of these experiences and have not wrestled yourself away from its grasp, and you are still reading this book, you are doing so out of curiosity, not because you need reassurance. If you have not had an ecstatic interlude of the sort I shall describe shortly, then the fact that others have had it, as William James notes, need not convince you of anything. Still, it may offer some reassurance.

Chapter 6

ARE WE A NATION OF MYSTICS?

UNTIL THE DAY HE DIED, BLAISE PASCAL, THE FRENCH
philosopher, carried on his person the words he wrote after
his conversion experience:

> From about half past ten in the evening to
>   about half an hour after midnight.
>   Fire.
> God of Abraham, God of Isaac, God of Jacob,
> Not the God of philosophers and scholars.
> Absolute Certainty: Beyond reason.
>   Joy.   Peace.
> Forgetfulness of the world and everything
>   but God.
> The world has not known thee,
>   but I have known thee.
>   Joy! joy! joy! tears of joy![1]

John Buchan, novelist and Governor General of Canada,
and as Scottish as Pascal was French, described a similar
experience:

> I had been ploughing all day in the black dust of the
> Lichtenburg roads, and had come very late to a place
> called the Eye of Malmani—Malmani Oog—the
> spring of a river which presently loses itself in the
> Kalahari. We watered our horses and went supperless
> to bed. Next morning I bathed in one of the Malmani
> pools—and icy cold it was—and then basked in the

early sunshine while breakfast was cooking. The water made a pleasant music, and nearby was a covert of willows filled with singing birds. Then and there came on me the hour of revelation, when, though savagely hungry, I forgot about breakfast. Scents, sights, and sounds blended into a harmony so perfect that it transcended human expression, even human thought. It was like a glimpse of the peace of eternity.[2]

F. C. Happold, a contemporary of Buchan and a writer and educator, also described such an overwhelming experience:

It happened in my room in Peterhouse on the evening of 1 February, 1913, when I was an undergraduate at Cambridge. If I say that Christ came to me I should be using conventional words which would carry no precise meaning; for Christ comes to men and women in different ways. When I tried to record the experience at the time I used the imagery of the vision of the Holy Grail; it seemed to me to be like that. There was, however, no sensible vision. There was just the room, with its shabby furniture and the fire burning in the grate and the red-shaded lamp on the table. But the room was filled by a Presence, which in a strange way was both about me and within me, like light or warmth. I was overwhelmingly possessed by Someone who was not myself, and yet I felt I was more myself than I had ever been before. I was filled with an intense happiness, and almost unbearable joy, such as I had never known before and have never known since. And over all was a deep sense of peace and security and certainty.[3]

Such extraordinary experiences—intense, overwhelming, indescribable—are recorded at every time in history and in every place on the globe and, as we shall argue later, are widespread, almost commonplace, in American society today. In times past, Joan of Arc had such an experience before leading her army into battle; St. Paul was knocked off his horse by a flash of light; Jesus apparently had at least two such experiences—at the time of his temptation and on Mount Tabor; the Buddha and Mohammed began their religious preaching after such interludes; the shamans of the Indian tribes of the Central Plains and the dancers of Bali go into mystic trances; Thomas Aquinas, just 700 years ago, described his life work as "straw" (*mihi videtur ut pavia*) after an intense ecstatic experience, and died, almost gladly, a few months thereafter; Abraham Lincoln may have had an intense mystical experience between the death of his son and the signing of the Emancipation Proclamation; Juan de la Cruz wrote his haunting lines in prison: "Upon a gloomy night, / With all my cares in loving ardours flushed, / (O venture of delight!) / With nobody in sight / I went abroad when all my house was hushed;" G. K. Chesterton describes an ecstatic trance in front of a toy shop window; Paul Claudel saw the whole of reality converge by a pillar in the cathedral of Notre Dame de Paris at the first vespers of Christmas.

But wherever the place and whatever the trigger and whoever the person, there run through the accounts of such interludes certain common themes—joy, light, peace, fire, warmth, unity, certainty, confidence, rebirth. Easterner and Westerner, saint and sinner, man and woman, young and old, all seem to report a virtually identical experience—intense, overpowering joy which seemed literally to lift them out of themselves (in some instances the ecstatics thought they could actually see themselves from the outside).

No one with any familiarity with history of anthropology or psychology can deny that such events occur. They are a form of "altered states of consciousness"—to use the currently approved phrase—something like intoxication, or delirium, or a hypnotic trance, but different in their intensity, their joyfulness and their "lifting out" dimension. In some cases, such experiences were triggered by drugs, in others by ritual dances, in still others by disciplined meditation; but most such "ecstatic interludes" about which we have accounts seem to be purely spontaneous.

Such intense and overwhelming experiences of peace, joy, unity, light, fire, love, confidence, and happiness turn up occasionally in the biographies of great men and women, but such events are easily dismissed as rare and perhaps bizarre episodes in the lives of the gifted, intense, and probably very neurotic people. However, such profoundly skeptical writers as Karl Mannheim, Sigmund Freud and Bertrand Russell have commented on the existence of these "occanic" feelings. Freud, who never had such an experience himself, was interested in them and included in his book *Civilization and Its Discontents* a description of an experience of his friend Romain Rolland: "A peculiar feeling, which never leaves him personally, a feeling which he would like to call a sensation of 'eternity,' a feeling as of something limitless, unbounded, something 'oceanic.' It is purely subjective experience, not an article of belief. . . ."[4]

The best known study of ecstasy is still *The Varieties of Religious Experience* by William James. He characterizes such experiences as "ineffable" (defying expression), "noetic" (providing an overwhelming experience of understanding), "transient" (lasting but a short time, although the "afterglow" may persist a lifetime) and "passive" (the person feels "grasped" by some sort of superior power).

James himself did not know what to make of these experiences. He was too careful a scholar to write ecstatics off as madmen, but too skeptical an agnostic to accept their testimony that the world was as benign and as joyous as they perceived it. Toward the end of his book, he offered a cautious concluding judgment: "Nonmystics are under no obligation to acknowledge in mystical states a superior authority conferred on them by their intrinsic nature. Yet . . . the existence of mystical states absolutely overthrows the pretension of nonmystical states to be the sole and ultimate dictator of what we may believe."[5]

The mainstream of psychoanalytic writing on ecstatic episodes is much less gentle. Its contention is that the mystical experience is a form of regression. It is "life schizophrenia," an "escape from reality." Stimulated by a severe "life crisis," an unacceptable external reality, one retreats to the world of infancy where one can deal with (or bypass) frustration and disappointment through an intense sensate experience. The mystic is a neurotic, a misfit, an incipient psychotic; he cannot cope with the real world, so he flees to one of make-believe.

The verdict is not unanimous. The psychologist Abraham Maslow thought that "peak experiences" or "core experiences" were benign and healthy. Some psychologists who have identified with the counterculture suggest that ecstasy induced by drugs or fasting or contemplation or self-hypnotism may be a means of personal growth. But it is still fair to say on the basis of the published literature that most psychologists tend to think that ecstatic episodes are either bizarre evidence of a disturbed personality or a potentially dangerous search for novelty among unbalanced young people in the counterculture. Most Americans would doubtless go along with such judgments.

When William McCready and I first began to think about our research into mysticism, we discovered that while we were thoroughly unmystical ourselves, a few people we knew had experienced such episodes. On the whole, they did not seem to us to be schizophrenic personalities or even any more neurotic than the general run. So, motivated by no more elaborate theoretical concern than curiosity, we managed to find room in a representative national survey of ultimate values among some 1,500 American adults for a handful of questions on mystical experience. We wondered how many people in American society have had "mystical" or "oceanic" experiences, what kinds of people are likely to have them, and what impact these episodes have on their lives.

At first blush it may seem just a trifle mad to use the techniques of a national sample survey to fathom the unfathomable, explain the inexplicable, eff the ineffable; but we would argue that the national sample may be the only way to begin the study of mystical experiences in modern society. There is no other technique to determine how often and to whom such experiences happen. Those mystics who are discovered by a national survey are likely to be very different from the college freshman who volunteers for psychological experimentation or the wandering mystic who drops into a researcher's laboratory.

Furthermore, artificially induced ecstatic experiences produced by drugs or contemplatic exercises or the various kinds of hypnotism or "mysticism machines" now being used in some laboratories are not necessarily the same things as the spontaneous experiences our respondents report. The basic difference between a spontaneous ecstatic interlude and one induced by a hallucinogenic drug, for example, is that one is induced by a drug and the other is not. However similar they may seem to be, they differ in that one critical respect at least. It may turn out that laboratory experiences and "natural" ones are indeed similar, but the only way that can be established is to study those who have had natural experiences.

We limited our investigation to those who reported having solitary mystical experiences. Group mystical experiences may occur in some segments of the population, such as young people living in community, but these communities are hard to ferret out with existing sampling techniques and are not typical of the national population, which was our basic interest.

The toughest problem was to figure out how to ask the question. Do you just walk into people's homes and ask them if they have ever had a "religio-mystical experience"? We did in one of our pretests and 50 percent of the respondents said they had. Our instincts—on which all question-worders rely heavily in the survey game—suggested that this might be too high a proportion. Another try was to ask whether they had ever felt as though they had become completely one with God or the universe. About 45 percent insisted they had. Finally, we settled on a question which seemed to reflect what the mysticism literature described as the core of the experience: Have you ever had the feeling of being very close to a powerful spiritual force that seemed to lift you out of yourself?

About 600 persons—two-fifths of the 1,500 persons asked the question—reported having had at least one such experience. About 300 said they had had it several times, and 75 said they had had it often.

Does such a question really get at whether a person has had a "mystical experience" in the classic meaning of the word? Until further research is done, we cannot say for sure. Obviously, one has to know far more about the experience that an individual respondent has had than can be gleaned in a first-round exploration. No survey question is ever perfect and doubtless this one is in many respects inadequate. If there is more research on mysticism, whoever does it will probably find better ways to ask the question. On the other hand, someone has to ask the question for the first time or there will be nothing on which to improve.

But we are moderately hopeful that the wording of the question is accurate enough for our present exploratory purposes. Those who say "yes" to it report that they have had an experience of a powerful spiritual force which seemed to lift them out of themselves. This "lifting out" (*exsto*—I stand out—whence the word "ecstasy") seems to be characteristic of all the mystical experiences about which we have read in the literature. Furthermore, more than two-thirds of those who have had such experiences placed the experience at the top end of a seven-point intensity scale. We are then dealing with people who report an intense experience of being lifted out of themselves by a powerful spiritual force. More than this we cannot say. Even if some (many, most) of these experiences are not "mystical" in the classic sense of the word, it is nonetheless a striking phenomenon that a large segment of the population is prepared to report such an intense experience. Whatever the nature of that experience, and however much it might fit the definition of traditional mysticism, it is in itself worth investigating.

Since there was not the time nor the money to ask for a detailed description of each experience, we presented the respondents with two lists from which to check off answers. One list offered choices of what triggered the experience, and the other was what the experience was like. Sure enough, the pattern we anticipated did indeed emerge. "A feeling that I couldn't possibly describe was happening to me," "the sensation that my personality had been taken over by something much more powerful than I am," "a sense of a new life or living in a new world," and "a sense that I was being bathed in light" clustered together in a pattern, which we called the "twice-born" factor. The principal relationships I discuss in the rest of this chapter are precisely with those "mystics" who scored high on the scale we created from this pattern, the "twice-born" factor.

We have, then, a substantial segment of the American population who have had intense spiritual experiences. We cannot now prove with certainty that they are all mystics, but we can ask what kind of people have such intense spiritual experiences. To suspend judgment on whether these are "real" mystical experiences, I will put quotes around the word "mystical" for the remaining portion of this chapter.

Who are the ones who have "mystical" experiences? People in their 40's and 50's are somewhat more likely to report "mystical" interludes than those in their teens. Protestants are more likely to experience them than Jews, and Jews more likely than Catholics. Within the Protestant denominations, it is not the fundamentalists who are the most frequent "mystics" but the Episcopalians (more than half of them). And within the two major denominational groups, the Irish are more likely than their co-religionists (be they Protestant or Catholic) to be "mystics."

Who are those who have these episodes often? They are disproportionately black, disproportionately college-educated, disproportionately above the $10,000-a-year income level, and disproportionately Protestant.

They are not the socially or economically disadvantaged in our society. If our ecstatics are running from anything, it is not from their social condition; and while "mystics" are disproportionately black, it is not the poor blacks but the college-educated ones who are most likely to have had such experiences. Furthermore, the "mystics" have positive and happy recollections of their childhood; they report close relations between their mothers and fathers and between themselves and each of their parents. They also report a religious approach by their fathers and mothers that was characterized by "joyousness." (Apparently it is the father's religious joyousness in particular which predicts ecstatic experiences in the child.) Finally, the whites who had such experiences are less likely to be racially prejudiced.

Most of our "mystics"—though not all—are religious in the sense that they are affiliated with one of the major denominations and they attend church, but there is a tendency for them not to be "churchy." They also seem to have an extremely strong sense of confidence in life after death.

There is nothing on the surface, then, which would indicate that the ecstatics are deprived or disturbed either socially or psychologically. One would have liked, of course, to administer complex personality tests or to attempt in-depth clinical interviews, but these are prohibitively

expensive techniques. We did administer the brief Psychological Well-Being Scale developed by Professor Norman
Bradburn. The relationship between frequent ecstatic experiences and psychological well-being was .40, the highest
correlation, according to Bradburn, he has ever observed
with his scale. We tried to explain away or at least to
diminish the strength of this correlation by taking into
account a number of variables (education, sex, age, race)
that might be responsible for it. The result was that the
correlation remained virtually unchanged, declining only
to .39.

We confess to being somewhat dismayed when professional colleagues dismiss our findings with an abrupt
certainty: "Those people can't be having religious experiences." Maybe not, but they're having something; and
whatever it is they are having, it correlates with mental
health at a very high level. If we had found any other
correlate, the mental-health establishment would be knocking down our doors demanding to know more. If anything
else but "ecstasy" were that good for you, it would sell as
if it wouldn't be on the market next year.

There is something stark and unsatisfying about a table,
a correlation coefficient, a factor loading. Perhaps one can
be content with such unromantic numbers when one is
studying political behavior; but it is hard—even for the
convinced survey-freak—to settle for numbers when one is
studying something as spectacular and bizarre as "ecstasy."
We would dearly love to have heard respondents tell us in
their own words what their experiences were like, but such
techniques would have been extremely costly. We had to
be content with our numbers—though, as we shall report
shortly, we did find some "mystics" to interview. Unfortu-

nately, they are completely unrepresentative. But their own words are still extremely interesting.

When our research findings became known to colleagues and friends, we encountered intense skepticism. One reviewer of an article we submitted to a professional journal accused us of trying to "bamboozle" the social science fraternity. A referee from another journal dismissed our findings as impossible and misleading. Representatives of funding agencies listened politely when we proposed further research, but shook their heads. The market was down and there were so many important things to study. We thought the funding agencies responsible for mental health research would be intrigued by the strong correlation between ecstasy and mental health. It turned out they simply didn't believe us. Such scientific objectivity is intriguing.

A second group of friends and colleagues did not deny our competence, our honesty or our objectivity; but almost as soon as they heard our findings, they eagerly searched for "natural" explanations—tachycardia, electrical discharges in the nervous system, a concatenation of lows or highs in the various biological cycles, a particular constellation of personality characteristics, inherited shapes of nerve endings, dietary deficiencies, fatigue, etc.

This kind of response at first baffled us because we did not argue, and do not argue, that there is anything "supernatural" about ecstatic interludes. As social scientists, we are concerned about the prevalence and incidence, the correlates and antecedents of such episodes—who has them, how often, what impact they have on their lives. We make no leap from those concerns to questions of whether such interludes "prove" anything about God or about the supernatural. Our stance was, and is, that we would leave the metaphysics, the theology and the perceptual psychology of these episodes to metaphysicians, theologians and perceptual psychologists. We stand with William James and say only that these are cognitive experiences which are interesting as such. They do not necessarily tell us anything about the ultimate nature of the cosmos. It is curious that so many of our colleagues felt compelled to refute the claims of special revelatory power for these cognitive interludes. We never made such claims.

(Both investigators in this study are part of that rapidly vanishing minority of believing and practicing Catholic Christians. But such a religious posture is not dependent on ecstatic experience at all—our own or anyone else's. Anyone who has had such an experience or who has read about them must decide for himself whether the universe is as benign, as gracious, as joy-producing as the mystic says it is. The evidence is inconclusive. The "mystic" may be right or he may be wrong; his cognitive experience may be a hint of an explanation or it may be self-deception. We believe in graciousness; we also believe that the only contribution research on "mystical" experience can make to the ultimate issue of whether the universe is gracious or not is to sharpen the question. If our data are accurate, we would estimate that, given the educational level of readers of this book, perhaps as many as half of them have had episodes of the sort we are measuring. We also would bet on the basis of our personal interviews that most of them have never discussed the experience with anyone else.)

A third reaction was the opposite of the two others. Friends and professional colleagues began to drift into the office, write letters and telephone with, "Say, I wonder if you'd be interested in some experiences I've had. . . ."

Colleagues could remain absolutely silent at a seminar while others expressed polite and occasionally not so polite skepticism about our data, and then come up afterward to us in the corridor and detail really spectacular ecstatic episodes. We fear the secret must be let out: Even at one of the world's most empirical places, the National Opinion Research Center, there are "mystics" on the loose, and they are not completely absent from the senior positions. Heaven only knows, but there are probably some around William James Hall at Harvard University.

We also discovered that at any social gathering we need only raise the subject of our research to find at least one person in the group who has had ecstatic experiences. At first, we simply enjoyed this phenomenon because it promptly shut up the skeptics; now we are also pleased with the information provided by these very unsystematic interviews, since it puts flesh on the bones of our statistical findings. From a few more than 20 such random interviews we have made a number of conclusions which could serve as the basis for further research:

(1) Like the mystics of the classic tradition, the interviewees perceived the phenomenon as fundamentally cognitive. They *saw*—not a person or a vision necessarily—the "way things really are." The core of the event is *knowing* something or Something. The joy, peace, heat, light and other such aspects of the experience are perceived as the result of the "knowledge." The truth of what they "know" is unshakable conviction, even if they are not able to put such truth into precise language that would have any meaning for those who have never experienced like episodes. "It is like a rose blooming in the snow, and my life has never been the same since."

(2) Virtually all of the respondents have never spoken about their experiences to anyone—spouse, friends, family, clergyman. When a discussion of statistical research on the subject "legitimizes" talk about it, the revelation comes as something utterly astonishing even to those who know the person well. "Why didn't you tell me about it before?" Least of all does one talk about it to a clergyman. One woman remarked that she could not even mention it to her brother, who was one, because, as she said, the clergy simply don't believe in those things any more, and he would want her to see a psychiatrist.

(3) Some of the episodes are spontaneous, with no apparent "trigger." Others are occasioned by clearly defined triggers, some of them crisis situations of the sort that psychoanalytic writers postulate, but others not. "I was sitting in the window studying for an exam, and the whole world poured in on me."

(4) Some experiences are overwhelming in intensity. Joy, confidence, heat, light, fire, laughter, enthusiasm are so powerful as almost to sweep the one caught by such an experience off his feet. To cope with such intensity requires a fair amount of ego strength and support from those around one. We suspect that many who end up on a psychiatrist's couch may be those who cannot cope with such intense experiences. Hence the analysts form their conclusions of the phenomenon from a very biased sample. Other experiences, however, may be much more gentle—powerful, indeed, but subtle rather than overwhelming. "I stood on the pier, looking at the stars and everything was so peaceful it seemed like I was in eternity and it would never end."

Some of the respondents can't remember *not* having

"mystical" experiences, while others seem to have had them only once or twice. But both groups insist that the experience was either the most important thing that ever happened in their lives or one of the most important things; that they have shaped their behavior and many of their decisions on the basis of the experience. Interestingly enough, no one to whom we have spoken wants such experiences again; they are astonished that some people might deliberately seek them. Ecstatic interludes are glorious when they happen, and they are critically important to the people who have them, but they are disconcerting, disruptive, disturbing. It is as though people are saying, "Thanks, but no thanks." One person told us, "It was so joyful that it hurt; I don't ever want it to happen again. I couldn't stand such pain, and I couldn't stand the worse pain of it stopping."

(5) We encountered a number of people for whom sexual intercourse was the "trigger" of their ecstatic interlude (about 20 percent of the sample). These respondents agreed that, while their experience was occasioned by orgasm, it was categorically different from orgasmic pleasure and much more powerful. As far as we know, the explicit sexual trigger has been noted only once before—by Marghanita Laski in her book, *Ecstasy*. "I had just settled into the 'afterglow.'" said one interviewee, "when something else happened which made the pleasure of that almost perfect lovemaking seem almost not to matter. I was possessed by something or someone whose demands made my very sexy partner seem dull and uninteresting. I was scared silly and thought I would lose my mind with pleasure." Perhaps the reason such scant attention is paid to such a trigger is that, in the Western tradition, most of the "mystics" who wrote about their experiences for us were celibate (though they certainly used passionate sexual imagery to describe the event).

(6) The people we interviewed were, with one exception, all "religious" in the broad sense of the word, though many of them were not "churchy." We asked one person who had no formal religious affiliation and was an infrequent church attender what he thought about the question of human survival after death. He responded, "I don't have any explicit or verbal answer to that question. All I know is that, once you have experiences like I've had [he had had two of them], the question doesn't seem very important. You know things will be all right, and you don't bother yourself worrying about details."

(7) There is a curious loss of time perspective associated with the ecstatic interlude. "Time stands still" is a phrase we heard frequently. Hours seem like seconds, or a few moments like hours. It is during that period of time confusion, apparently, that the unity and convergence of all things are perceived. One respondent told us how he frequently walks down to a pier jutting into a small lake of an evening and the next thing he knows it's sunrise. Another described her sister finding her in church several hours after she had gone in, though it seemed to her only a few moments had passed. John Brodie, the articulate, sophisticated former quarterback for the San Francisco 49ers, has described a phenomenon of time lag when dropping back to throw a pass.

(8) For all but one of the respondents, the experience was benign. In the one exception, the structure of the experience was the same: Time stood still, the universe was perceived as converging, one's place in it was clearly specified. But the universe in this instance was hostile, vindictive; and instead of joy and peace, the person experienced what he called "cosmic buzz." We were able to tease out of our national survey some evidence of similar phenomena, which

we called "dark night" mysticism. (It is more like the dark night of the senses of classical mysticism than the dark night of the soul with its more specifically religious connotation.) Those who have such experiences seem most likely to be from unreligious backgrounds and from fairly aloof and reserved family relationships. "If God is responsible for those things," said our agnostic respondent, "I don't want any part of him. He is Ingmar Bergman's spider."

(9) All of the respondents were creative, happy, dynamic individuals, though we would hesitate to say whether their creative proclivities were a cause or effect of their ecstatic episodes (or neither). One might say of most of them that they were intense individuals, but on the basis of their career performances and achievements, as well as the quality of their relationships with family and friends, the intensity seemed constructive rather than neurotic. "What the hell," said one young woman, "you gotta do something till it or he or she or whoever or whatever it is gets around to coming back again."

(10) There seems to be some relationship which we have not yet been able to understand between "mystical" experience and consciousness of death. We use the word "consciousness" advisedly, because we are not disposed to say our interviewees are more afraid of death. They are more aware of death, but this awareness does not seem to be morbid. As one very active young woman put it, "I am not afraid of death, but it's very much on my mind. Sometimes to think about it makes me relaxed and peaceful."

(11) A "sudden death" experience has triggered "mystical" interludes for some of our interviewees. Their descriptions parallel the pattern recorded by sudden death

researchers—the rapid turnover of anger, life passing in review, resignation, peace, serenity, and then ecstatic joy (and the next thing you know, you're in a snowbank and have to study for the final examinations after all). In "The Accident," G. K. Chesterton describes with characteristic flair one such event in his life on the occasion of a runaway hansom:

> But in those few moments, while my cab was tearing toward the traffic of the Strand, . . . I really did have, in that short and shrieking period, a rapid succession of a number of fundamental points of view. I had, so to speak, about five religions in almost as many seconds. My first religion was pure Paganism, which among sincere men is more shortly described as extreme fear. Then there succeeded a state of mind which is quite real, but for which no proper name has ever been found. The ancients called it Stoicism, and I think it must be what some German lunatics mean (if they mean anything) when they talk about Pessimism. It was an empty and open acceptance of the thing that happens—as if one had got beyond the value of it. And then, curiously enough, came a very strong contrary feeling—that things mattered very much indeed, and yet that they were something more than tragic. It was a feeling, not that life was unimportant, but that life was much too important ever to be anything but life. I hope that this was Christianity. At any rate, it occurred at the moment when we went crash into the omnibus. [*The Accident, Selected Essays of G. K. Chesterton.* London: Collins, 1936, p. 68.]

Again, we don't know what to make of this phenomenon. It may be merely an evolutionary adaptation by which certain human beings who are better able to cope with death are more likely to survive and reproduce than those who are terrorized into powerlessness at the threat of death.

If we are forced to depart from our sociological agnosticism—as well as our own woeful inexperience—and to try to guess what really happens in "mystical" interludes, we would say that we think they are episodes of intense and immediate cognition in which the total personality of a person is absorbed in an intimate though transient relationship with the basic forces, cycles, and mechanisms at work in the universe and in his own psychosomatic composite—gravity, cosmic rays, light, heat, electromagnetism, cycles of breathing, circulation, digestion, day, year, life, death.

We are all inextricably caught up in those various ongoing processes but hardly ever notice them, much less "break through" to their harmonious interaction. The "mystic," we think, intuits all of these things at work in a single all-encompassing insight. The capacity for such comprehensive, intense, and transient knowledge is probably latent in all of us, but for reasons of nature or nurture, it is likely to be stronger in some than in others. We have no explanation why the experience is almost always joyous—save that the universe or the universal forces (or "being," if one wishes to be philosophical) seem to be intuited in these interludes as gracious and benign.

Both our representative national sample and our random personal interviews seem to suggest that ecstatic episodes are relatively frequent in American society; and for most people they are positive, constructive, and healthy, though sometimes they are so intense that those who have them are not eager to go through such an experience again. What conclusions would we draw from such findings?

First, we submit what all researchers submit, that there

ought to be more research. It is indeed interesting that a phenomenon as widespread as "mystical" experiences apparently are has been almost totally ignored and unstudied by social scientists. We think the churches have been even more remiss in not paying attention to intense religious experience. None of our respondents had discussed his or her ecstatic interludes with the clergy. One put it, "I knew it had to do with God and religion; but I didn't think it had anything to do with the church." It may be that in their passion to be "with it," church leaders have missed those kinds of people who are "with" something that is at the core of all religion.

We also conclude that the mental-health workers ought to be much more cautious than they are in equating such experiences with schizophrenia. Doubtless some "visionaries" are schizophrenic, but our data strongly suggest that others are not. Some personalities, however, seem ill-equipped to cope with such intense joy. They need support from mental-health workers; the implicit hint that they are nothing but schizophrenics could easily turn them into schizophrenics. We asked one man, whose wife went into an extraordinarily powerful ecstatic episode after an afternoon's lovemaking, what he thought was happening. "Well," said this Jesuit-trained Chicago Slav, "I figured she was having a mystical experience.I thought it was nice, but I didn't know who was going to put the kids to bed or make my lunch the next morning." And how did he react? By helping. He did those chores himself. His wife quickly added that if it hadn't been for this combination of support and down-to-earth realism, she might have ended up in the hospital. Not all those who find themselves "surprised by joy" (to use C. S. Lewis's words) are so lucky.

Most mystics, it would seem, are humans whose hope has become so overwhelming that it has taken possession of their personality. You can argue with them if you will, you can tell them that they have no scientific evidence, no solid proof, and that you do not have to believe them. The mystic will shrug his shoulders. You are well within your rights not to believe him, but what he knows, he *knows*. The mystic's testimony is the same as the testimony of the paradise poets of the world religions I quoted in a previous chapter. It cannot be so persuasive as to eliminate all our doubts. On the other hand, their testimony is so strong that if we have rejected life after death, they make us uncomfortable in that rejection. The testimony of the mystics forces the skeptic to doubt his skepticism.

"DESCRIPTORS" OF MYSTICAL EXPERIENCE
FOR THOSE WHO HAVE HAD ONE OR MORE

"Descriptor"	Per Cent
A feeling of deep and profound peace	55
A certainty that all things would work out for the good	48
Sense of my own need to contribute to others	43
A conviction that love is at the center of everything	43
Sense of joy and laughter	43
An experience of great emotional intensity	38
A great increase in my understanding and knowledge	32
A sense of the unity of everything and my own part in it	29
A sense of a new life or living in a new world	27
A confidence in my own personal survival	27
A feeling that I couldn't possibly describe what was happening to me	26
The sense that all the universe is alive	25
The sensation that my personality has been taken over by something much more powerful than I am	24
A sense of tremendous personal expansion, either psychological or physical	22
A sensation of warmth or fire	22
A sense of being alone	19
A loss of concern about worldly problems	19
A sense that I was being bathed in light	14
A feeling of desolation	8
Something else	4

Chapter 7

LIFE BEFORE DEATH

THE REASSURANCE PART OF THIS VOLUME NOW COMES TO AN end and we come to the meditation part. It may be that the ecstatics and the saints do not require reassurance on the subject of human survival, but most of the rest of us do. We may believe the revelation of the Easter experience, but we still need reassurance. A book on life after death which passes over the reassurance issue will be unsatisfactory and unhelpful. I have assembled what reassurance I can from an analysis of human hopefulness, from a sociological report on the relative stability of beliefs after death, the fascinating research of the wonder sciences, and from the persistence of mystical experience among contemporary Americans. As I have said before, these reassurances are not designed to "prove" but merely to reassure. Proof is by the nature of these things impossible.

But if we have been reassured, the question for our daily lives is how should we live? If one has been grasped by the Easter phenomenon, if one has been illumined by the light of the Christian spring festival, when one has danced in the Christian rite of spring and sung the *Exsultet* with faith and conviction, then what?

Note that this is not an apologetic issue. It is an issue of the Christian life, of ascetics, if you wish to rely on the old division of the theological and religious disciplines. It is not a discussion about the validity of the Christian worldview but of how people live who have been grasped by that worldview and are committed to it.

I am often asked as a priest what kind of "arguments" I use to persuade young people that premarital sex is wrong. My usual response is that it depends on who the young people are. If they are nominal Christians and not totally committed to the Christian worldview (and such, indeed, is the state of most young people), then I give them the standard arguments about the risks and dangers in promiscuity. A moderately persuasive case can be made on humanistic psychological grounds against premarital sex, but I do not know how effective those arguments are with young people caught in the power of youthful passion. My suspicion is that it is not normally very effective. Should they succumb, I am not inclined to believe that they are thereby cut off from the loving concern of the God Jesus revealed to us, who, fortunately, was neither a moral theologian nor a canon lawyer.

If the young people involved are thoroughly committed Christians, then I drop the psychological hokus pocus and say that it is the message of the gospel and the tradition of the Christian community that followers of Jesus of Nazareth don't do that sort of thing. The appropriate question, in other words, for those who explicitly and self-consciously believe the revelation of God in Jesus is not what is sinful and why is it sinful and how sinful is it, but how do we who are followers of Jesus behave?

I was once severely taken to task in the public domain by a priest who thought that this was an arrogant, simplistic, and harsh way of thinking. I fear that somehow he thought there was a judgmental aspect to my position, that I was pronouncing "mortal sin" on all kinds of people. Perhaps it was a failure of communication on my part, or perhaps the "mortal sin" mentality has been so prevalent among us that we see it even where it is explicitly excluded. In any case, the ascetical question, "How do the followers of Jesus of Nazareth live?" has rather little to do, I think, with the old "works of superarrogation," or the "evangelical councils," or "the quest for perfection" of the spirituality of not so long ago. (Although the original insights behind such terms *may* have been an attempt to convey the same thing I am talking about.)

For the convinced Christian the important question is not what is sinful and what is not, or even what is virtuous but not required. The pertinent question is how do I live in such a way that I celebrate the gospel I believe in? Is my life a celebration? If I am filled with flaws, imperfections, mistakes and errors, I am not thereby committing a sin; I am just something less than a perfect Christian. No one is a perfect Christian. I need not feel guilty for my failures. When I fail to live the life of radiant hopefulness that is appropriate for a Christian, I ought to be disappointed in myself, but I am not and will not feel guilty in either a psychological or theological sense. The Christian life, in other words, is not so much an obligation imposed from the outside as a mode of behavior that is imposed naturally and logically—though often with great difficulty—from the vision of faith that is ours.

The issue is not moral behavior, which falls under obligation and wins approval for us; the issue is the extent to which our personality is permeated by the vision of faith that we experience in our grasp of and our being grasped by the resurrection of Jesus. To what extent does the Christian spring ritual which is reenacted each day at mass, as well as in special fashion during Easter season, dominate our life? To put the matter yet another way, to what extent are we ready to give free rein to the powerful, surging forces of hopefulness that are latent in our personalities? We live the Christian life to the extent that our hopefulness is unchained and freed from the constraints and restrictions that our cynicism, anxieties, and fears impose upon us. Any description of the Christian life, such as the one contained in the Sermon on the Mount, is not meant to be either moral obligation or ascetical counsel. It is intended to provide a set of criteria by which we are able to judge how much our hope has been liberated from the bonds of fear which restrain it. The criteria exists not as perfection which we are obliged to attain, but as a goal, an ideal toward which we strive or, even better, a model by which we can evaluate our efforts. Again I would emphasize that the efforts are not so much toward achieving something as toward releasing something that is already latent in us.

Non-Christian and even Christian theologians who are skittish about belief in life after death frequently argue that the doctrine is used by Christians as a pretext for dodging the responsibilities of this world and of this life. In order to give the secular its full due value, they say, one must eliminate the belief in another world to which one can flee after suffering the necessary injustices and oppressions of this one. Life after death is nothing more than pie in the sky when you die. If your treasure or your reward is some where else, then you won't give this world full effort. You will accept oppression and misery as part of a divine plan, indeed as means to merit glory in another life.

The critics may have a point. There is a certain kind of Christian piety which denies the value of things worldly, indeed uses the term "worldly" in the most pejorative sense. From the viewpoint of this piety, the only thing for a good Christian to do is to flee from the world and all its pleasures, demands, challenges, and responsibilities by going·off into the desert to find salvation. It is also doubtless the case that much social injustice has been justified on the grounds of the transient nature of this life. There has been a tendency in Catholic piety to treat sexuality in marriage as a necessary evil to be conceded to those who lack the strength and courage to choose a better and more perfect way. There have been far too many Catholic Christians who have thought that all life is about is the "salvation of the soul," and that this is achieved largely by performing ritual and ascetical acts—the more the merrier. One saves one's soul by piling up a strong positive balance on the ledger sheet that the Great Accountant in the sky is keeping. One avoids sin and performs certain acts of virtue, particularly the kind which win indulgences; and since social, economic, and political activity are not indulgences, these things are scarcely appropriate ways to earn one's "eternal salvation." For such people, it may well be conceded that life after death is a cop-out from the responsibilities of life before death. Furthermore, such salvation-obsessed people, so confident that they have a heavy balance in the Great Ledger Book in the Sky, can be difficult, nasty, and arrogant in their dealings with other human beings.

In fact, however, Christianity is not concerned with the salvation of the soul. Jesus did not preach salvation of the soul; he preached resurrection. The mark of the Christian, according to Jesus in that decisive 25th chapter of St. Matthew, is not the performance of ascetical ritual acts but service to the least of the brothers and sisters. Furthermore,

St. Paul insists repeatedly that the material world is saved through human beings; it is not something evil, sinful, to be rejected. It is ripe for salvation. Christianity, like its Jewish relative, is a this-worldly religion concerned about service to the brothers and sisters in this world and the salvation of the whole cosmos in and through Christ Jesus. Those who have distorted Christianity to a "life after death" religion misunderstand completely the essence of the Christian worldview. We are not a life after death religion; we are a religion of the resurrection. Hence we do not reject the human body or the world of which it is a part. On the contrary, we believe both are of immense value because they are destined for resurrection. We are deeply and fundamentally concerned about the problems of this world and the problems of the human beings within it. Both the pie in the sky crowd and their critics misunderstand Christianity in general and the Christian notion of "afterlife" in particular.

The assault of the "other-worldly" view of Christianity by the secular theologians has been so powerful that one would almost not need to mention the subject if it were not for the fact that in very recent times there has been a resurgence of extremely fundamentalist religious perspectives. The other-worldly distortion of Christianity is suddenly turning up in the most unexpected and even fashionable places. It is also worth noting, in passing at least, that Christianity is not simply a this-worldly religion either. Some of the secular theologians, Protestant and Catholic alike, are so concerned about making their point of the importance of "this world" that they almost seem to deny the existence of anything transcendent. It is a long step from saying that this world is valuable to saying that the only valuable things are to be found in this world. It is still a step which a number of enthusiastic theologians seem to be unable to make, particularly when they insist that any question of what happens to the human personality after death is not only irrelevant but actually impedes Christian service in this world.

In fact just the opposite seems to be the case. For if one destroys human hopefulness or dismisses it as irrelevant, then one is likely to be faced with a collection of zombies, who, having little confidence in their own future, see no reason why they should be concerned about that of anyone else either here and now or in future generations. As Robert Heilbroner has put it, "Why should I worry about the unborn?" And Heilbroner has been able to answer the question. As a product of three thousand years of Jewish and Christian tradition, he feels he ought to be concerned about them, but as a practical pagan, he can't think of any good reason. In fact, most people who have not been influenced by the Jewish and Christian worldviews see no particular reason why they should be concerned about correcting social injustice much less worry about the unborn. It is presently fashionable to be critical of economic and scientific progress, and now Christianity is blamed for fostering it. (Christianity used to be blamed for opposing it.) It is true that not only the economic, technical and scientific progress in the Western world but also the political, social and cultural progress take their origins in the extraordinary thrust toward growth and development that Christian hopefulness introduced into the human condition. Doubtless, sometimes this growth got out of hand and did much more harm than good, though on balance the human race is probably much better off without Justinian's Plague, the Black Death, or the Spanish Influenza.

Some theologians manage to have it both ways. They blame the Christian belief in life after death for the non-involvement of Christians in worldly problems, and they blame Christian hopefulness for the economic and scientific progress which has produced a good number of our problems. And all the while they do not credit any Christian sense of social justice revealed in Matthew 25 or the Christian conviction of the dignity of each individual person, with providing the principles and viewpoint from which virtually all Western social criticism is based.

You just can't win.

For our purposes it is sufficient to say that however one might blame Christianity and for whatever one might blame it, the true follower of Jesus of Nazareth is every bit as concerned as he was about the social and moral problems of his age—and Jesus was deeply concerned, as one can tell from even the most cursory reading of the Bible. Christianity is neither a this-wordly nor an other-worldly religion; it is a combination of both. It is a religion that believes in divine action in human history. The Transcendent is working out His purposes in this world, and so both this world and the otherworld are of critical importance, each revealing and reflecting the importance of the other. God revealed Himself in history, and by that very fact, the importance of human events is revealed. If God is at work in this world, so must we be. If the Transcendent is involved in our world, then our world is somehow or other destined for transcendence. The Christian lives in both worlds simultaneously, and it is in the tension between the two worlds that the dynamism of Christian hopefulness is released.

If there was merely a life after death in some other world totally unrelated to this one, then we might be dispensed from commitment to the problems and responsibilities of this world. And if that life after death consisted merely of the life of a disembodied soul, then the problems and concerns of this world and the bodies that live in it would be irrelevant. But Christianity believes that this world and the other interpenetrate (and the quintessential focus of this interpenetration is, of course, the revelation of God in Jesus which we call the Incarnation). It also believes not in the survival of a disembodied psyche after death but rather in resurrection in which the whole human person continues to live, body and soul together; and with and in the survival of the human body the whole cosmos will also survive. We look forward, as the epistle of St. Peter says, to new heavens and new earths, by which he meant a renewed heaven and a renewed earth. How this is to be achieved, of course, is far beyond the purview of the epistle's author. More simply, the Christian does not believe in life after death; he believes in life. As G. K. Chesterton puts it, he believes that life is too important ever to be anything else but life. Any life that persists after death cannot be discontinuous with this life. The Christian believes in the continuity of life. Death is not the end of an old life and the beginning of a new one, it is a transition which may modify but does not change the fundamental flow of life. Death, as Frances Thompson has put it, is birth.

How do Christians who believe in resurrection live? First of all they are necessarily men and women of hope. Indeed, by definition they are men and women of hope because their experience of the resurrection has unleashed their hopefulness which transforms the whole of life. We do not deny the existence of suffering and evil in the world; we are not Pollyannas, prettying over life so that all its raw ugliness is obscured. We do not think that everything will turn out all right in the short run or even the middle run; we are merely convinced that all will be well in the ultimate run. We know that sickness, suffering, and death are the lot of humankind; but we work fervently, diligently, and enthusiastically while there is still light because we know that death does not have the final word. This dear, sweet, precious life that we have is stronger than the death that threatens to snuff it out. We do not go silent into Dylan Thomas' good night, but neither do we rage, rage against the failing of the light, because we know that the night is truly good and that the light, however dim it may get, will ultimately never fail. We do not like to grow old; we do not like the grim milestones of the various life turning points of thirty, forty, fifty; we do not like to have our bodily strength weaken and fail; we do not like to grow weary and discouraged, battered and beaten with life's frustrations. But we have something more than Gail Sheehy's advice in *New York Magazine* to face them "openly and honestly."

Death is not the end of life; it is the experience of being cut off from Being. When we die it seems that not only our life ends but that we cease to be. We move into nonexistence, our being is annihilated. Theologically this may be restated as the fear of being cut off from God. The death fear enters our lives very early, as the psychoanalysts have made clear. It is the fear of being cut off, of being alienated permanently. The Christian conviction of resurrection, experienced in the Easter symbol and ritual, says that nothing can cut us off from the love of God which is in Christ Jesus.

We do not know very much about what happens after death
—though as we shall see in the next chapter, it is possible
to speculate. The core of the Christian resurrection experience is the conviction, unshakable and irrefutable, that
nothing can cut us off from God's love. Or, as one of my
colleagues who has had two intense mystical experiences
puts it, "I don't know whether I believe in life after death,
but once you have experienced what I have experienced you
know that everything will be all right, that there is nothing
to worry about, that the goodness which you have experienced will take care of you. In the face of that overwhelming goodness, questions about immortality seem almost
trivial."

And they are "almost trivial" not because the question of
human survival is trivial but because the goodness of whatever is Ultimate is so overwhelmingly obvious that one is
quite prepared to leave the final disposition of things in the
hands of that Gracious Ultimate, knowing that however
things work out, they will be far, far better than we could
possibly imagine. The resurrection of Jesus tells us that
nothing can cut us off from that Ultimate Graciousness.
From one point of view that may seem like a rather minimal
belief. Nothing can cut us off from God's love. Is that all?
Is there nothing more to Christianity? The only response
possible is, "What more could there possibly be?"

Does this hopefulness make a difference in the way we
live? McCready designed a series of vignettes to measure
"ultimate worldview" of our survey respondents. We presented them with situations concerning their own death, the
death of loved ones, a natural disaster, the birth of a handicapped child, and asked them how they would react. We
sorted out a number of different patterns: "religious opti-

mism," or religious fundamentalism, which defined the problem of evil out of existence "secular optimism," which argued that everything would work out for the best somehow, "anger," which presented Dylan Thomas' position, though in a much less poetic way, "resignation," a passive acceptance of one's fate, and "hopefulness," which looked at evil without denying its reality yet asserting that it did not have the final word.

We assumed that "hopefulness" was the Christian response to evil.

It turned out that hopefulness did indeed have an impact on the way people lived, and that even with educational levels held constant, hopeful people were much more likely to have high scores on racial and religious tolerance than anyone else. It does indeed matter what you believe about the way things ultimately are and the way things ultimately will be.[1]

The hopeful person, then, is one who survives because he believes in survival; he lives because he believes in life; and he celebrates because he believes he has something worth celebrating. He can afford to be more tolerant of others because others are less likely to threaten him. Diversity is not a challenge to his individuality or his freedom because he knows that nothing can really destroy that which is most uniquely and essentially himself. He is perhaps not any less afraid of death; we are all afraid of death. But he is not paralyzed by that fear, he will give up and quit, anticipating death by dying psychologically and humanly long before he dies physically. The hopeful person dies only once. He lives strongly and vitally up to the point of death.

Hopefulness does not preclude discouragement, disillusion, frustration; it does preclude bitterness and cynicism.

Hopefulness does not mean that we do not fall; but it does mean that we get up and walk on. Hopefulness says with T. S. Eliot, "Disillusion if persisted in is the ultimate illusion." Life is not a bowl of cherries, it is not a picnic, or even a parade; it is, quite literally, a deadly serious business. It is so serious that a Christian, obsessed as he is by hope, has no choice but to laugh about it. He says with Gregory Baum that "tomorrow will be different, even if tomorrow is the day after the last day of our lives." It may well rain on today's parade, but let's see about tomorrow.

And this expectation for what tomorrow may bring is the final, most special, most distinctive aspect of the Christian "life before death." The Christian is curious, he wonders about tomorrow, he is intrigued by its possibilities and fundamentally unafraid of its terrors. John Shea has written that the best way a Christian can prepare for death is to develop a healthy capacity for surprise. It seems to me that that is the best description of the Christian life I have ever read. We are engaged in the business of developing our capacity for surprise. No matter how worn or weary or battered or frustrated or tired we may be, we still have an ability to wonder; we are still open, curious, expectant, waiting to be surprised. What will be around that next corner? Who lurks behind that bush? What is that Cheshire cat smile that just vanished in the leaves of yonder tree? Who is that knocking at the door? Who is messing around the garden? Who is trying to peek in through the latticework? Who is that making all the noise, leaping and bounding around over there in the hills? What's going on here? Is there some kind of conspiracy, some kind of plot? Who is the Plotter? There is something mysterious about this house. There's a Ghost in it, and he just went down the corridor. What the hell is going to happen next?

Ultimately, then, the universe is either an empty machine held together by some clever but essential brute force, or it is a haunted house spooked by playful ghosts. In the machine there is no wonder or mystery; in the haunted house there are a thousand puzzles, lots of tricks, and a surprise a minute. The best ghost stories are always comedies, so there is also a laugh a minute. Like Thomas More, we may even die laughing.

So the Christian goes to bed at night not afraid that he will wake up tomorrow to find himself dead, but curious as to what crazy fool surprise lays in store for him when he wakes up in this sometimes frightening, sometimes absurd, sometimes even vicious but always fascinating haunted house of a world.

Or, to sum up the whole Christian argument, how do we know that tomorrow will be different? Every other tomorrow we have known has been different. Why shouldn't the next one?

Chapter 8

LIFE AFTER DEATH

"AND YOU ARE LYING ON THE BEACH," INTONED THE HYP-
notist-analyst in her rich Viennese accent, "and you are at
peace. Six angels appear, and they are strong, handsome
angels with great wings and flowing white robes. They lift
you up, up, up into the air, and you are transported up into
the sky, through the clouds into heaven."

By now I was deep in the trance, and the hypnotist's
power of suggestion was receding into the background. My
own unconscious was taking over. The angels lost their
wings, their white robes, and their angelic faces, appearing
in rough brown and green garments. And they weren't
carrying me; we were striding down a forest road on a spring
morning, singing great marching songs as we went and
laughing as we sang. We came to a top of a knoll, and
there the forest ended. We looked out over a great, sprawl-
ing city which did not, to tell the truth, look anything like
the book of Revelations. It glittered white in the sun,
indeed, but it was no mysterious Oriental city. It was a
great, bustling, modern metropolis with skyscrapers and
rapid transit and moving vehicles and streams of people
moving to and fro. Beyond its towering skyline there glittered a great, smooth blue lake. It was a place, my vigorous
escorts informed me, to which I could not go quite yet, but
they assured me that it was there; and it was a great,
splendid city, was it not? Perhaps the most striking thing

in the city was its activity. I would not call it frantic, but it was alive with activity. It glittered not with rich marble or soft pastels but with sharp, bright, active, vital colors. Slowly the vision receded and I rose out of the trance.

"But a very strange thing happened," said the hypnotist, "when the angels were lifting you into the sky you were solemn and serious, and you had a very 'religious' look on your face. But then when you were deep into the trance the look changed, and it was almost as though what you saw was funny, almost as though you were enjoying a great joke. Indeed you had the expression of a little boy who is doing something very wicked by delightfully watching something he wasn't supposed to see at all. It did not seem to me," she concluded, "to be a very religious experience for you at all."

I guess it depends on what you mean by religious. It clearly was not a vision of floating around on clouds with winged, white-robed, harp-playing angels. It was not a glorious Byzantine city all solemn and sacred in gold and marble. If you believe that God is a comedian and the Holy Spirit is a leprechaun, you can't think of heaven as a very solemn, sober, and dull place.

I am sure that when my unconscious took over I combined Robin Hood's merry men tramping through Sherwood Forest with my first sight of San Francisco from the Twin Peaks and Chicago's lakefront seen at sunrise on a clear spring morning. That, at least, is what my unconscious thinks heaven is like, and on balance it strikes me that it couldn't be any better.

But imagine your own heaven if you will. If it is to be a Christian heaven, you can dispense with the Greek image of people sitting around plucking musical instruments and not doing much else but look vapid. The Christian heaven is active, dynamic, vigorous. It is not a place where life ends but rather a place where it continues.

In one sense it is not at all difficult to imagine what life after death will be like, for it will be, as I have argued repeatedly in this book, like life as we know it here on earth. It will be filled with the excitement, the wonder, the pleasures, the activity that makes life rewarding and exciting here on earth. Any sharp discontinuity between the two forms of life is completely foreign, I think, to the Christian resurrection symbolism. It was the same Jesus on Easter as before, transformed perhaps, glorious perhaps, but still Jesus. So it is with us, we believe, and the transformation will destroy nothing that is good or true or beautiful about human life. On the contrary, it will merely enhance what we already are.

On the other hand, we cannot even begin to imagine what our continued life will be like. Jesus himself has told us this: "Eye has not seen, nor has ear heard, nor has it entered into the heart of man those things which God has prepared for those who love Him." Our expectations, according to Maeterlinck, are all too modest. It will be life as we know it here on earth, but so transformed that we cannot even begin to imagine how splendid it will be. "Dream your most impossible dreams, hope your wildest hopes, fantasize your most impossible fantasies," Jesus tells us. "Then where they leave off, the surprises of my heavenly Father will only begin."

So we can look forward to both continuity and discontinuity, continuity of life but extraordinary transformation of the quality, the intensity, the richness, the splendor of life. It sounds like quite a show.

Most certainly this continued life of ours will be marked by surprises and by wonder. It is hard to imagine any kind of human life without surprises and wonder. If we have lost the little child's capacity to delight in surprise, to be awed by the wonder, we have not become adult; we have become aged and senile. The fullness of life requires a highly sensitive awareness of the possibility of surprise and a powerful capacity for wonder. If life persistent is to be life at all, then it must be life filled with surprises and wonder. John Shea's comment that the Christian prepares for death by developing his capacity for surprise is strictly and literally true. One simply cannot make it in the heavenly kingdom unless one is able to cope with surprise. Perhaps that's what Purgatory is all about; it's a place where we are given the chance to make up for the sense of wonder we did not develop and the capacity for surprise that we permitted to atrophy here on earth. Purgatory would then be less a place of suffering and more a place of preparation, a kind of spring training camp where we can learn to enjoy the wonderful, the marvelous, the unexpected.

Will hopefulness continue in the heavenly kingdom? I have argued throughout this book that that which is most authentically human in us is our hope. It is what enables us, forces us, to ask the religious questions and gives us the most powerful hint we have of the religious answers. It is that which most enables us to be ourselves, to release the full, rich, and vigorous potentialities of our personality, to take risks, to ask not why, but why not?

Will we have dispensed with hope when we come to the many mansions of the heavenly Father's kingdom?

The old catechetics said that we would, arguing that when one has achieved one's goal there is nothing left to hope for. Certainly St. Paul implied as much in his famous quotation in the first epistle to the Corinthians, chapter 13.

If one restricts hope to the human ability to assert that death is not the final answer, that when all the evil things that are possible have been done to us there is still yet one more word to be said, then obviously there is no more need for hope after that answer and after that last word. But hope can also mean a confidence of further growth, development, expansion, a challenge to more activity, a readiness for new adventures, an openness to new wonders. It is very hard to see how there can be human life without this kind of hope. So hope in this sense, or, as the sociologists would say, some kind of functional substitute for what we would call hope in our present state of life, would surely persist in our continued life after the transition point of death.

On the psychological level, I would suggest that what we will experience in our continued life will be what my colleague Mihaly Csikszentmihalyi calls "flow." He means that experience we enjoy when our capacities and talents are pushed to the limits but not beyond them. We experience "flow" not when we are doing something easy and routine, which requires little interest and generates little excitement, nor when we are doing something that is beyond our capacities and overwhelms us with complexities and demands. Rather we experience "flow" when we exercise the full vigor of our powers, when it is demanded of us that we do our best. Csikszentmihalyi describes how chess, sports, mountain climbing, surgery can all be "flow" activities for those who are skilled in them. It is almost as though an "automatic pilot" takes over, and one does what one must do with a rich, full, enjoyment, reveling in the challenge and one's capacity to meet it.[1]

I experience "flow" when I write, particularly when I know what I want to say, when I have command of the data and resources that I need, and when the whole article or book appears in my mind's eye laid out as a coherent, unified system. I need only to commit myself to the onflowing process of producing the book; the experience is neither dull nor overwhelming but challenging, satisfying. I can do what I am called on to do by the project, and I can do it with ease and skill (regardless of what the reviewers might say), but also with the full satisfaction that comes from knowing that one's abilities are being pushed to their limits.

It happens again for me on water skis (a safe and secure pair). Give me a strong motor, a fast boat, a good driver and a smooth lake and I can give myself over completely to the joyous rhythm of wind, air, water, and blades slicing across wakes. One plunges into the rhythm and is taken up by it, and without conscious thought or reflection, one weaves back and forth in a spontaneous, playful exercise of one's skills (which in my case happen to be moderate at best). Off to one side, back across the wake, off to the other side, weaving, spinning, turning, shifting the tow rope from hand to hand, not afraid of falling (foolishly, perhaps), but alert every second to the possibilities and challenges of the endlessly shifting environment of air and water in which one finds oneself. Muscles straining yet relaxed, wind beating fiercely but not painfully against the skin, one becomes unself-consciously part of the environment, bending with it, leaning on it, pitting one's resources against it, and enjoying every glorious second.

I also experience "flow" when sailing, especially in an offshore wind which produces a brisk and steady movement without high waves to endanger my fragile *Leprechaun*.

Sailing for me is much like skiing, although it adds the
extra dimension of the tension between sail, rope, and wind.
I am not much of a sailor, but flow experiences need not
require great skills; they only require situations which de-
mand the best of the skills we have. One man's "flow" is
another man's boredom and another's terror. If you are one
of that rare breed who has climbed the Himalayas, then
the small mountains in upstate New York will be boring.
If you have never climbed a mountain at all, the upstate
New York peaks might well be terrifying. And if you are a
modest, beginning climber, wrestling the peak in New
York to submission might be just within your capacities and
can easily result in a "flow" experience for you.

Each of us can think of our own "flow" experiences.
Tennis, golf, cooking, singing, working with power tools
are some examples perhaps. My guess is that "flow" experiences, which abound in our daily lives, are the best
concrete, practical anticipations we get of what the delights
of the heavenly life might be.

It sounds like a pretty good deal.

If we want to turn to images, there are two I find
especially appropriate for describing the continuation of
our life. The first is Marc Connolly's superb play, *Green
Pastures*, in which the Lord God becomes a black southern
Baptist preacher, the angel Gabriel stands ready, horn in
hand, for the Great Day, and all the citizens enjoy an
endless picnic fish fry. *Green Pastures* is out of fashion
now; it is written off as an "Uncle Tom" play. The religion
of American blacks, we are informed, was simply one of the
tools of white oppression, and *Green Pastures* is an expression of those techniques devised to oppress blacks. (In
fact, research by Eugene Genovese and Timothy Smith

show that black religion was anything but a means of oppression. It was, on the contrary, a way of keeping human dignity alive in the face of incredible obstacles, and more a source of resistance and even rebellion than for passive acceptance of tyranny.)

St. Brigid had the same idea. Heaven was a place where there would be a great pool of ale:

I should like to have a great pool of ale for the King of Kings; I should like the Heavenly Host to be drinking it for all eternity.

I should like to have the fruit of Faith, of pure devotion; I should like to have the couches of Holiness in my house.

I should like to have the mead of Heaven in my own dwelling; I should like the vats of Long-Suffering to be at their disposal.

I should like to have the vessels of Charity to dispense; I should like to have the pitchers of Mercy for their company.

I should like to have the Three Marys of glorious renown: I should like to have the people of Heaven from every side.

I should like to be vassal to the Lord; if I should suffer distress he would grant me a good blessing.

"I Should Like to Have a Great Pool of Ale." 10th Century. Translator Kenneth Jackson. In *An Anthology of Irish Literature, Volume I*, David Greene, Editor. New York: New York University Press, 1971, p. 32.

Get the picture: An Irish king (anyone with more than
ten head of cattle) and his henchmen have been walking
across the countryside in the cold rain and fog (it's never
any other weather there). They finally arrive at the castle
(a long wooden hut, to tell the truth) where they are to
visit another king (this one has fifteen head of cattle—truly
a great lord). They enter the castle wet, weary, hungry,
discouraged. There is food and drink and the singing of
songs and the telling of tales, and a grand good time will
be had by all as the night wears on. Of course, as it comes
closer to morning, the singing grows more spirited and the
tales more spectacular, and the good time even better. "Ah,
isn't it grand, boys!"

This vision of the Lord God presiding over a grand Irish
drinking party is profoundly offensive to all kinds of pious
souls—including, alas, some with Celtic names who ought
therefore to know better. Archbishop O'Dwyer, for example, in a rather nasty editorial in *The Register* pleaded
with me to spare the befuddled Catholic laity images of
God presiding over a drinking party. (Though, paradoxi-
cally, the archbishop seems to like St. Brigid's poem, which
pictures just that. To tell the truth, I have a feeling it's
just me he doesn't like.)[2]

The fish fry and the Irish feis, those occasions of the
singing of songs and the telling of tales, are profoundly
offensive to puritans, dullards, wet blankets, and party
poopers. How dare one suggest that heaven is like that?

Well, neither Marc Connolly, St. Brigid, nor I thought
the idea up. There was someone who once said, "The
kingdom of heaven is like a great banquet." And again he
said, "The kingdom of heaven is like a marriage feast."
What the hell (one should excuse the expression) is a great

banquet or a marriage feast unless it's a crashing good party? There is a paradox, of course, in the notion of heaven/wedding banquet or heaven/party; but that is the nature of the parable style of Jesus. Sharp, contrasting pictures are pushed together to create surprise, wonder, tension. "Heaven" meant one kind of thing to his listeners and "party" meant something quite different. You put "heaven" and "party" together and you have limit-language, language which both records and triggers a limit-experience, which forces us to say, "Oh *that's* what he's talking about!"

Continued life, continued excitement, wonder, surprise, challenge, "flow," smashing great parties—those are the kinds of ordinary human experiences which best enable us, I think, to anticipate what our continued life will be. We can, of course, spend too much time reflecting on it. The temptation to go back into my trance (an activity I am much better at, it turns out, than waterskiing) and investigate my marvelous mixture of Sherwood Forest, San Francisco, and Chicago is quite strong. But there are other things to be about. We prepare for the life that is to come not by fantasizing about it but by living hopefully, joyously, "flowingly," wonderfully in the present life. We prepare for the permanent resurrection festival by celebrating resurrection in the here and now. Each time we run the risk of dying to the old self so that we might rise to the new, we not only anticipate but we participate in that which is to come.

I am not by nature a celebrating person. I was well into the middle years of life before I was able to enjoy parties—and now I enjoy them far more when I am giving them. (How about that for a strong taint of the Protestant ethic!) Furthermore, I abhor parties in which I am the only sober person present, and I am strongly tempted to put my fist through the teeth of the occasional drunks who dare to mess up my parties. (And sober type that I am, I remember the next morning just what has been said by the drunks —something which no gentleman does, I am told.) Still, there is something terribly wrong if we cannot celebrate easily, joyously, spontaneously, without the benefit of four or five drinks. Celebration ought to be a characteristic of our lives. Not for nothing is the clergyman presiding over the mass called a celebrant. Alas, no better evidence do we have of the sorry state to which the Church has fallen that so many of our celebrants are party poopers both in the way they say mass and in their behavior outside of mass. Consider, for example, the dour and somber clothes that canon law imposes on the clergy—black, which tradition tells us is supposed to represent the shroud in which the cleric will be buried. Clerical garb is supposed to warn both the cleric and his people of the inevitability of death. One would have thought that they were all well aware of that, and what the garb of the clergyman ought to signify is not the inevitability of death but the triumph of life. In this respect, at least, the hierarchy in their purples and reds, crimsons and whites, far more adequately represent the kingdom of heaven.

As two little children of one of my Jewish colleagues remarked of my appearance one day, "You look scary!"

Celebrant indeed.

The kingdom of heaven is a perpetual spring festival, celebrating, as do all spring festivals, the persistence of life as life, triumphing, however painfully, over death.

Woe to you party poopers and wet blankets, for you shall not enter into the kingdom of heaven—not without a long time in Purgatory, learning how to wonder, how to be surprised, how to celebrate.

And blessed are you who celebrate despite your tears, for yours is the kingdom of heaven.

NOTES

Chapter 2

1. See, for example, Schubert Ogden's *Reality of God, and Other Essays*, New York: Harper & Row, 1966; and Stan Stenson, *Sense and Nonsense in Religion*, Nashville, Tenn.: Abingdon Press, 1969.

Chapter 3

1. *The Collected Poems of G. K. Chesterton*, New York: Dodd, Mead & Company, 1966, pp. 199–200.

2. Anonymous French folk rhyme in Jacques Choron, *Death and Modern Man*, New York: Macmillan and Company, 1964, p. 161.

3. Choron, p. 161, from Jean Finot, *La philosophy de la longévité* (The Philosophy of Longevity). Paris: Felix Alcan, 1902, p. 253.

4. F. C. S. Schiller, *The Riddle of the Sphinx*. London: Macmillan & Co., 1912, p. 380.

5. Bertrand Russell, "A Free Man's Worship," in *Mysticism and Logic*. New York: Doubleday (Anchor Books), 1957, pp. 44–45.

6. Max Scheler, *Schriften aus dem Nachlass*. (Posthumous Writings). Berne: Franke, 1933, Vol. I, "Tod und Fortleben" (Death and Survival), p. 407.

7. Elisabeth Kubler-Ross, *On Death and Dying*, New York: Macmillan & Co., 1969, paperback edition, 1970, p. 139.

8. The Pharisees, who developed more strongly than any other in Second Temple Judaism the notion of a personal relationship between humans and God, logically concluded that God could not permit a human with whom he was in love to perish. Hence the resurrection came into Jewish religious thinking through the Pharisees. In this respect, as in many others, Jesus was firmly in the Pharisaic camp. Indeed it is no exaggeration to say that Christianity is a Pharisaic Jewish sect. The bad press the Pharisees receive in some parts of the New Testament is based on a situation which existed after the time

of Jesus to some extent. It also seems likely that the Pharisees were among the adamant opponents of Jesus. However, Phariseeism, like the rest of Second Temple Judaism, was far more pluralistic than we had realized until very recently. Jesus himself was clearly in the tradition of the "Pharisees of love"— though he made substantial and decisive additions to that tradition.

9. Between the writing of the book of Job and the composition of the book of Maccabees, a striking revolution occurred in Jewish religious thought. Job agonized over the meaning of life, but the Torah religion of his ancestors seemed to give him no encouragement about the possibility of a life after death. However, the various compositions that were collected into the book of Job are to some extent conflicting on this subject, and the recent analysis based on the use of Ugaritic words seem to indicate that in some parts of Job there is a tentative belief in immortality.

However, by the time of the book of Maccabees, several hundred years later, there was not the slightest doubt that belief in immortality existed, at least among some segments of the Judaism of that day. We know relatively little of the dynamics of this change, though, as was mentioned earlier, the Pharisees were deeply involved in it—probably both as a cause and an effect. Surely, the notion of Yahweh, developed by such later prophets as Ezekiel and Jeremiah, as a God deeply involved in a personal relationship not merely as "the people" but now as individual humans, would not permit the individual human to be snuffed out permanently.

10. Stanzas 10–12 from Vedic funerary hymn, Rig Veda X, 18, translated by Ralph T. H. Griffith, in his *The Hymns of the Regveda*, IV (Benares, 1892), pp. 137–9; adapted by Mircea Eliade in *Death, Afterlife, and Eschatology* (Part 3 of *From Primitives to Zen*), New York: Harper & Row, 1974, paperback edition, p. 25.

11. Lines 95–98, 100 of *Menok i Khrat*, edited by Anklesaria. Translation by R. C. Zaehner, in his *The Teachings of the Magi*. London: George Allen and Unwin Ltd. and New York; the Macmillan Company, 1956, pp. 133–138. In Eliade, p. 43.

12. H. B. Alexander, *North American Mythology*, Boston:

Cooper Square Publishers, Inc., 1916, pp. 147–9; adapted from James Teit, *Traditions of the Thompson River Indians of British Columbia*, Boston and New York, 1898. In Eliade, p. 49.

13. Alfred Métraux, *The Native Tribes of Eastern Bolivia and Western Matto Grosso*, Bureau of American Ethnology, Bulletin 134 (Washington, D.C.), 1942, pp. 105–106.

14. *Sukhavativyuha*, ch. 15–17, 18. Translation by Edward Conze, in Conze et al., *Buddhist Texts through the Ages*, Oxford: Bruno Cassirer Ltd., 1954.

15. Translation by Arthur Jeffery, *Islam: Muhammad and His Religion*. New York: Liberal Arts Press, 1958, pp. 98–103; trans. from Ibn Makhlūf, Kitāb al'Ulūm al-fākhira fī'n-nazr fī Umur-al-Akhira (Cairo, 1317 A.H.-A.D. 1899), II, 151–153.

Chapter 4

1. The "other" category in American survey research represents approximately 3 per cent of the population. It includes such diverse groups as Ukranian Orthodox Catholics who refuse to be categorized as "Roman," Anglo-Catholics who reject the terminology "Protestant," and fundamentalist denominations eager to distinguish themselves from mainline Protestants, as well as Mormons, Orientals, and other small groups.

2. We were badly handicapped by the fact that we were unable to ask our respondents any more than whether they had had such experiences. It would be important to know the quality of the experience, whether it occurred in a waking state, whether there was conversation with the dead person, whether anyone else was present, whether the dead person was actually seen or his presence sensed, whether the respondent felt that it was an extraordinary "supernatural" event or merely a strange feeling. Also, how did the 25 per cent reporting such contact interpret the adverb "really"?

Chapter 5

1. See the fine book *A Contemporary Meditation on Hope* (Thomas More Press) by Father John Heagle. I read the book only after having written the previous chapters of this volume, and was struck by the convergence of our two approaches.

2. The wonder sciences are not occult in the sense that

this word has come to be used in recent years. On the contrary, the wonder scientists are terribly embarrassed by the interest in their disciplines manifested by the cultists of the occult. They attempt to study the marvelous, indeed, but their studies are carried out in the broad light of day by the most refined of scientific methods. They are not engaged in muttering incantations by candlelight or brewing herbs and potions.

In reading the words of the wonder scientists, however, one must constantly test their skepticism. The will to believe in one's findings is universal to the scientific enterprise, of course. If forgeries have been found recently in the parapsychological disciplines, they have also been found in more traditional ones too. One becomes involved especially in proving one's point when others deny it out of hand. Credulity is by no means a monopoly of the wonder disciplines. Still, one must be especially wary of it when one is pursuing the literature.

3. Karlis Osis, "Some Frontiers in Survival Research," *Spiritual Frontiers,* Volumes 6 and 7, numbers 4 and 1 (Autumn and Winter 1974) pp. 98–99.

4. Michael Polyani has pointed out that it is inevitable in any human intellectual enterprise that there will grow up an established view of the way things are. Findings that do not agree with such a view are set aside or ignored in the hopes that they will eventually be refuted. Or as one psychologist remarked to me, "Even if ESP were proved, I still would not believe it because of what it would force me to acknowledge about the rest of the universe."

5. When McCready and I casually decided to throw in some questions about paranormal experiences in one of our surveys, we were urged by a friend to include a question about "out of body" experiences. I rejected such a suggestion out of hand—most nonscientifically, as it turned out. Subsequent conversations and reading of the literature have persuaded me, however, that such experiences are apparently rather frequent and have been scientifically documented in the sensory deprivation experiments. One study of undergraduates at Oxford University revealed that a third of the sample reported one such phenomenon. McCready and I are now preparing to ask a question about out of body experiences on a national sample survey.

142 DEATH & BEYOND

6. The Soviets seem to have a much more open mind about their psychological research, and seem much more willing to invest money in it than we are.

7. For a detailed report on the Kirlian photographic phenomenon, see S. Ostrander and L. Shroeder, *Psychic Discoveries behind the Iron Curtain*, Englewood Cliffs, N.J.: Prentice-Hall & Co., 1971.

8. I omit from this discussion an account of the work of Michel Gauquelian, a French scientist from Strasbourg, who has amassed a vast and interesting body of evidence about the impact of cosmic conditions (location of moon, sun, and stars) on behavior. Gauquelian's research does not demonstrate the validity of astrology but it does show that the ancients who took the astrological phenomena seriously may not have been complete fools. For a discussion of this research and of psychic operations on the island of Lusanne, and a wide variety of other wonder science phenomena, see the two books by Lyall Watson, *Supernature* and *The Romeo Error*. Watson, a biologist, combines to an impressive extent an open mind and strong skepticism.

9. *In Parapsychological Monographs No. 8*, New York: Parapsychology Foundation, 1969, p. 63.

10. The initials used to describe "psychokinesis" or the ability of the human mind to have an impact on the physical environment without using the ordinary means of establishing contact between the person and the environment. Some parapsychological laboratory experiments have apparently established the existence of such phenomena.

11. Proceedings of the Society for Psychical Research, Vol. normal Phenomena, Science, and Life after Death," in *Parapsychological Monographs* No. 8, 1969, published by the Parapsychology Foundation, Inc., 29 West 57th St., New York, N.Y. 10019, pp. 31–32.

12. *ESP Reader*, David C. Knight, Ed., New York, Grosset & Dunlap, 1969.

13. Lyall Watson, *The Romeo Error: A Matter of Life and Death*, pp. 113–114. New York, 1975. Doubleday & Co. (Anchor Pr.)

14. *Ibid.*, p. 115.

15. Incidentally, the persistence of this energy field could solve a problem for those Catholic theologians who quite rightly insist that a disembodied "soul" is not a human person, and that for humanity there must be some linkage to the physical universe. The energy field would presumably represent such a link. The problem then becomes a question of whether the physical energy field can subsist for long independent of the body which generated it.

16. Watson, p. 156.

Chapter 6

1. Quoted by F. C. Happold, *Mysticism: A Study and Anthology*. Middlesex England: Penguin Books Ltd., 1964, a Pelican original, p. 39.

2. Happold, p. 131. Quoted from John Buchan, *Memory Hold-the-Door*. London: Hodder and Stoughton.

3. Happold, *op. cit.*, pp. 133–134.

4. Sigmund Freud, *Civilization and Its Discontents*. Longdon: Horgarth Press, 1953, pp. 7–8.

5. William James, *The Varieties of Religious Experience*. New York: The New American Library, a Mentor Book, 1958.

Chapter 7

1. Curiously enough, we encountered the same skepticism about this finding that we did about the research on mysticism described in the previous chapter. Many professional colleagues can see no point in McCready's questions and are not inclined to use them in surveys even though he has demonstrated conclusively a fairly high relationship between world view and racial and religious attitudes. Being more patient than I, or younger, or perhaps more hopeful, McCready does not seem incensed by this skepticism.

Chapter 8

1. See his forthcoming book from the Josey-Bass Press.

2. He made a crack in the editorial about my having written the column in question when I took time off from asking

Catholic women whether they took birth control pills—a question which, incidentally, we have never asked in any of our surveys. When we meet at the great heavenly bash, I hope the archbishop will have the good taste to admit that I was right.